Alexei Sayle's

GREAT BUS JOURNEYS OF THE WORLD

Alexei Sayle's

GREAT BUS JOURNEYS OF THE WORLD

Alexei Sayle and David Stafford

Methuen

First published in Great Britain 1988
by Methuen London
First published in this paperback edition in 1989
by Methuen London
Michelin House, 81 Fulham Road, London sw3 6rb
Copyright © Alexei Sayle and David Stafford 1988

Reprinted 1989

Designed by Julian Dorr

Typeset by Rowland Phototypesetting Limited
Bury St Edmunds, Suffolk
Printed and bound in Great Britain by
Richard Clay Limited, Bungay, Suffolk

A CIP catalogue record for this book
is available from the British Library
ISBN 0 413 62670 9

Contents

Many thanks to Don Atyeo and Maria Lexton at *Time Out* and Richard Holledge, Mike Molloy and Geoff Garvey at the *Sunday Mirror*.

Great Bus Journeys of the World

If you ever have to appear as a defendant in the law courts – perhaps for contravening Gladstone's 1856 Spitting Act or for being in breach of the EEC Molestation of Jelly, Blancmange or Edible Sauce Laws – something that has happened to me not as often as some people say – then your brief, your barrister, always tells you to wear a smart suit, to cut your hair, to clip your nails and so on, in order that you don't upset the judge whose idea of an innocent person seems to be someone who's just spent two hundred pounds in Top Shop. But this just isn't right. It is your actions that are being tried, after all, not your dress sense. A person should be able to appear in court dressed as a chicken or with their underpants on their head if they want and it shouldn't affect the judge's decision on your case.

It was thus that I found myself facing the most severe Contempt of Court order in the history of British Justice and it was for that reason that my advisers suggested I make myself scarce for at least a year.

With this thought in mind I approached the editors of several learned magazines and up-market newspapers – all of whom were eager to employ my prodigious talents. I suggested to them an idea that I had been nursing for some time, that for a year I should travel the off-peak bus lanes of the world, that I should report back to them by means of weekly despatches, that they should print these despatches plus any correspondence that should arise and that they should give me a fuck of a lot of money.

The editors of these journals were uniformly enthusiastic about this undertaking.

And so as the new year dawned crisp and bright myself and the enigmatic David Stafford found ourselves – lavishly equipped with a quantity of comical tropical kit that we had bought in a shop in Piccadilly with the express purpose of writing funny stuff about – standing outside Golders Green station, waiting for the first number 28 of the year, waiting to begin the first of many journeys in which we would cross and recross the globe on that most unglamorous of conveyances – the humble bus!

7

JANUARY – ENGLAND

6.15a.m. London Regional Transport: Route 28 – Golders Green to Wandsworth via West Hampstead.

The bus was there but there was no sign of the crew. We sat on it for a bit, nothing happened so there was nothing to write about – disaster! In this travel writing game each moment has to be dripping with significance. I got off and wandered into the adjacent Northern Line tube station.

Hooray! My heart leapt. Nestling in a dark corner of the terminus was one of the most un-written about phenomena of modern times – a Photo-Me-Booth.

To you Photo-Me-Booths are just smelly boxes for having your photo took that you sometimes find in stations. But, stranger, look closer, for in truth they are much, much more: they are, in fact, gateways between one dimension and another, spanning the continuum of space and time – each booth straddles a crack in the very fabric of existence itself. Through this tear in the substance of the universe we are afforded a glimpse of another parallel world: behind the mirror on the wall of the Photo-Me-Booth there is another Earth, another Time.

Unfortunately life is much tougher, harder and more unpleasant in that other world and that is why after you have put your money in the machine, the photos that you get back are not of you but instead are of some sad-eyed and dispirited stranger who stares pleadingly back at you through the glass. One of the reasons life is dull in the other world is that it rains all the time which explains why your photos are always wet when you get them.

Also these bridges to the other dimension are unstable and are often prone to close, which goes some way to explaining why, when you want a passport photo and you go to a place where you are certain you've seen a Photo-Me-Booth, it isn't there any more.

However, all is not drabness in the world of the Photo-Me-Booth. For example, some of the most exciting and creative theatre work of the late seventies and early eighties was performed by the Photo-Me-Booth Theatre Company. The aim of this innovative troupe was to perform all the classics of Western Theatre in a Photo-Me-Booth by distilling the text into a maximum of the standard four passport-sized frames. Although in 1985 the group's three quarters of a million pounds Arts Council grant was cut and they went their separate ways, there thankfully still exists a definitive record of their work.

Photo-Me-Booth Theatre present their interpretation of Cats.

**"PHOTO-ME-BOOTH
THEATRE"**
Humbly Present
Their Production of

Les
Miserables

**20
Years
Later**

The Photo-Me-Booth Theatre's production of Les Misérables.

Towards the end of its career Robert Maxwell buys the Photo-Me-Booth Corporation and thereafter has to appear in every photo taken.

Having got all I was going to get out of the tube station I rambled outside again. The crewless bus still squatted on its stand. Humming to myself I strolled over to the other side of the road, espying one of those blue plaques that adorn the London buildings where famous people once lived. I looked closer. The circular plaque stated that the said building once housed the great Albanian poet, writer and thinker, Klepke Klepke. Again my heart leapt! The one volume that always accompanies me on my travels is Klepke

Klepke's towering semi-autobiographical book *Man of Soup*. Here was an ideal opportunity to reproduce some of it.

> 'Later, much later, I went to the café. The one we called 'Novac' joined us at this time. It was cruel of us to call him 'Novac' because he actually had a perfectly good Electrolux machine but he had run out of bags for it.
>
> One of Novac's drawbacks was that he entirely lacked imagination. He once wrote a book called *One Thing To Do With A Dead Cat,*
>
> Shortly before he died he was working on a new book, or rather a series of stories, called *Roget's Adventures of Tin-Tin*:

> 'Captain Haddock the mariner, sailor, sea–dog, seaman seafarer, salt, shellback, tar, looked, beheld, spied upon, observed, caught sight of, glimpsed at, viewed, witnessed, watched, gazed upon, stared at, peered at, noticed, scrutinised, inspected, contemplated, rubbernecked at Tin-Tin. "Blistering excrescence-filled, noded, emphy-semic, carbuncled, warty, vesticled, pustulent barnacles, whelks, crustacea, razor-shells, winkles, mussels, cockles, cephalods, lobsters, crabs, crayfish, langoustes, oysters, clams, whelks!" he said.'

Deep in thought I walked back to the bus stop. When I got there I found a deserted stand – in my absence the bus had left. I got a taxi home and went back to bed.

The Next Day – My House.

Embarking on a mammoth expedition like this takes a great deal of care and planning – most important of all, of course, is writing the spin-off book. To write it I've bought myself a portable word processor – I can type two hundred words a minute – mglm mefooy yipxxxxxxxxmallllollopppitty bosh. They don't make any fucking sense but I can type 'em!

There are also many attendant worries. Countless members of expeditions – polar explorers, jungle trekkers, mountain climbers – when they get together over mulled wine in the Explorers Club talk about a strange phenomenon which happens to a great many of them. When camped in some remote spot or climbing in a blizzard they are often struck by the curious sensation that there is one more member to the party than there actually is. On Scott's trip to the South Pole his diaries record that they constantly imagined there to be an extra person – they used to put an additional plate out for him and gave him a name. Now what's really weird is that I have had a slightly similar experience myself.

For many years now I have had the feeling that I've left something in the dry cleaners! I constantly suspect that I've dropped some article off at the twenty-four-hour laundry and then forgotten absolutely all about it.

I have learned to suppress this feeling, otherwise I would have to check in at the cleaners every day. Of course another explanation could be that some time ago, six years, maybe, I *did* leave something in a dry cleaners somewhere. Well, if I did, I hope it wasn't something that would go off – an Edam cheese or an elephant perhaps.

London Regional Transport: Route 24 – Hampstead Heath to Trafalgar Square via Camden Town.

The 24 bus route is a route steeped in historical and literary associations. Every schoolboy knows that this was the bus on which the Treaty of Versailles was finally ratified, but who now remembers that V. I. Lenin got his first experience of power while working as an inspector out of Chalk Farm Garage?

Lytton Strachey and Virginia Woolf were frequent travellers on the 24 bus. They would board at the top end of Tottenham Court Road and travel north to visit Strachey's Auntie Kathleen who was a dinner lady at All Soul's Primary School in Camden Town. Virginia's diaries bubble with excitement about the trip:

> Went to see Lytton's Auntie Kathleen again. We sat on the upper deck, as usual and, having told me about his latest ideas for *Eminent Victorians*, Lytton noticed that the front seats were vacant. Hurriedly we transferred to these seats and had a wonderful time pretending to 'drive' the bus. Lytton is such a talented man. His impersonations of bus noises, with authentic gear-changing sounds at the right moments, have to be heard to be believed. Got home about five o'clock. Cooked Leonard's dinner. Wrote *To The Lighthouse*. Bed.

Musical associations are almost too numerous to mention. Edward Elgar conceived the idea for a follow-up to his very successful Second Violin Concerto (the sadly unfinished Second Violin Concerto II) while waiting at the stop. Booker T (of Booker T and the MGs, whose recording of 'Green Onions' rocketed them to stardom in the early sixties,) conceived his idea for the literary prize also while waiting for a 24. At least five songs have been written about the bus route: Gershwin's 'A Foggy Day in Camden Town'; Bacharach and David's 'Twenty Four Bus Ride From Tulsa'; Manfred Mann's '5 . . 4 . . 3 . . 2 . . 24'; Talking Heads' 'Once in a Bus Ride'; and of course the Sex Pistols' 'Anarchy In The UK'.

William Randolph Hearst, the American press tycoon, loved the bus so much that he put in a bid to have the entire route transported, brick-by-brick, to California at a cost of $88 trillion – which in those days was a tidy sum.

But perhaps the most tragic moment in the history of this illustrious route was the fateful day in 1963 when John Fitzgerald Kennedy, travelling down Gower Street in an open-top 24, was assassinated by . . . will we ever know the truth? As Peter, Paul and Mary so aptly put it: 'Dragons live forever, but not so little boys.'

Many interviews these days concentrate not on what the interviewee has to say about their art but rather questions are asked about peripheral things such as choice of clothes, hobbies etc. Examples of this style are features like 'A Room of my Own' in the *Observer*, the *Standard*'s 'Ad Lib' column and the 'likes and dislikes' features in many teen chart mags. This is thought to be more interesting for the reader and may also tangentially throw light on the interviewee's work. Seeing as no one ever asks to interview me about anything at all I have been forced to introduce the Great Bus Journeys Celebrity's Questionnaire Interview, conducted on the top deck of a number 15 bus by a Sooty glove puppet.

SOOTY: So, Alexei, we don't see much of you in Britain these days but I hear you're really big in the States. Do you have a home over there?

ALEXEI: Yeah, I'm working on a pilot for a TV series in the States. It's a half hour sitcom based on *Merry Christmas Mr Lawrence*. I play the David Bowie part but I don't make it as funny as David did in the film, and the fat guy from *Cheers* plays the camp commandant. The midget from *Different Strokes* will guest from time to time as Lord Louis Mountbatten. I share an apartment in LA with Billy Idol. In LA I only hang around with people called Billy – Billy Idol, Billy Ocean and Billy Liddell who used to play for Liverpool in the late '50s.

SOOTY: Do you have any pets?

ALEXEI: Not exactly, but there's something living under the wallpaper that I'm a bit worried about.

SOOTY: What about your love life?

ALEXEI: My girl friend Amanda is a model. At the moment she's an Airfix kit of a Stuka dive bomber. She's also the Burmese Vice-Consul to the Court of St James. Most of our friends are Fleet Street journalists, the rest do experiments on live animals for a living. We go to the Hippodrome most nights, as I like people with low intelligence.

SOOTY: Many people have had a hand in my success, but who has helped you and which three things would you take to a desert island?

ALEXEI: Well, I'd take a stepladder, a spoon and a stuffed lobster. As to help, I guess I owe a lot to François Mitterand. He's a very special guy in many special ways, but I suppose I shouldn't say more than that.

BUS INSPECTOR: Excuse me, sir, can I see your ticket?

SOOTY: Here's mine, boss.

BUS INSPECTOR: Thank you. And you sir? Here! This disabled person's bus pass looks a bit suspect pal!

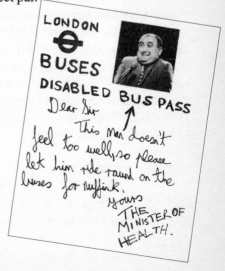

I'm afraid sir that I'll have to kick you downstairs.

ALEXEI: No! Ow! Ooooch! Klonk! Yike! Ugh! Crikey!

SOOTY: I'll stay on for a few stops if you don't mind.

Tavistock Hotel, Tavistock Square.

I settled back on the bed and got out my battered copy of Klepke Klepke's *Man of Soup* – as usual Albania's greatest writer had much to say about the condition of the artist.

Meanwhile, back at the café, Lovacs was still expounding his theories of art.

'The true artist,' he expounded, 'should always be open to experiences of all kinds. He should be at the same time a part of and yet separate from the outside world. He must work to keep his vision fresh. It is also unwise for him to eat the contents of a thermometer or sleep with a frozen turkey.'

We chaffed at Lovacs's ideas. Lovacs leapt to the defensive.

'They laughed at Arthur Askey!' he asserted. 'And history has proved them wrong.'

Suddenly Lucak woke up and told us his new theory of poetry. For years, he explained, the poet was constrained by the tyranny of rhyme. Meaning, feeling, thought, were all compromised by the crushing convention of perfect assonance. Attempts by the so-called modern school of poets to do away with rhyme have been met with jeers and catcalls. 'This is not poetry,' say the public. 'Where is the rhyme?'

Lucak explained that rhyme and freedom of expression could happily co-exist and, indeed, rhymes be made totally perfect if, instead of the ends of poetic lines merely rhyming, they ended with the same word. He gave an example:

There was a young lady from Dewsbury bollocks
Who went to the shop for some fish bollocks
As she walked in the door shit
The shopkeeper said shit
What kind of fish would you like bollocks?

This hotel is only about fifty yards from my house but now I am off on my expedition I can't return there for a year. I have given a great deal of thought to the kind of hotel I'll be staying at. During my early career as a stand-up comedian I was sometimes forced to stay in those small hotels called 'guest' houses. How do they find the people that run these places? Does somebody put an ad in the paper saying 'Wanted – mean-spirited petty tyrant, with an aversion to children, people, animals and joy – to run small hotel.'?

A lot of the rooms and corridors in these 'guest' houses seem to be adorned with neatly printed hand-written notices done in felt tip with lots of underlining giving various orders to the residents –

VISITORS ARE REMINDED
THAT FOOD MAY NOT
BE CONSUMED IN THE ROOMS

or

ON **NO ACCOUNT**
MUST CLOTHES BE
WASHED IN THE
BASINS OF ROOMS.

or

No Pets

or

No Smoking

or

```
+-------------------------------------------+
|                                           |
|   No Visitors                             |
|   ========================                |
|                                           |
+-------------------------------------------+
```

I could take everything else about these boarding houses – the nylon sheets and the glass bambis on top of the television but these signs brought out a rare resentment in me. On a wet weekday in the lounge of the Bide A Wee Cream Scone Guest House in Exeter something snapped. I crept out to the shops and returned some hours later, drawing card, pens, tape and pins hidden about my person. Over the next few weeks in the horrible hotels I stayed in I stuck up many of my own notices amongst the genuine ones. Mine were somewhat different in subject matter.

```
+-------------------------------------------+
|                                           |
|  VISITORS MUST                            |
|  KEEP A DEAD BADGER                       |
|  IN THE SINK AT ALL                       |
|            TIMES.                         |
|                                           |
+-------------------------------------------+
```

```
+-------------------------------------------+
|  IF THERE IS NO DEAD                      |
|  BADGER PLEASE OBTAIN                      |
|  ONE FROM RECEPTION.                      |
+-------------------------------------------+
```

or

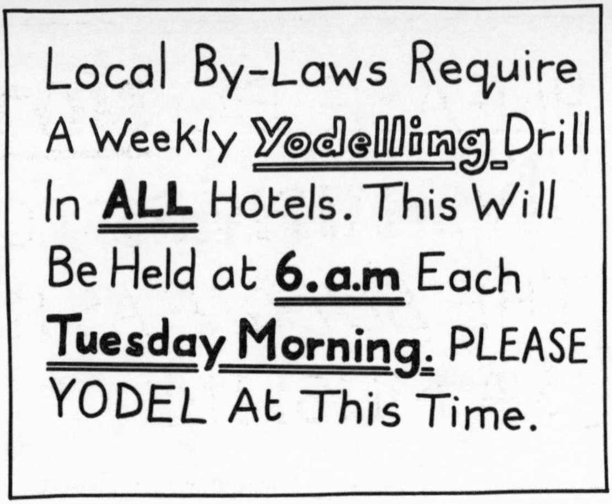

Local By-Laws Require
A Weekly _Yodelling_ Drill
In **ALL** Hotels. This Will
Be Held at **6.a.m** Each
Tuesday Morning. PLEASE
YODEL At This Time.

or

No Crocodiles

or

CHICKPEAS ➔

or

PLEASE DO **NOT** GIVE *KIPPERS* TO THE *BUDGIE* AS HE IS A MUSLIM.

FEBRUARY

*London to Paris with Captain Magic's Exploding Trouser
Bus Company.*

Captain Magic's Exploding Trouser Bus Company was started in
1968 by the legendary acid casualty 'Fizzing' Sid.

The bus company originally operated out of Blackpool and its first
trip was overland to Gorakpur by tram. The tram set off from outside
the Winter Gardens in a blaze of drugs: Pink Floyd records played
from its external speakers; balloons, streamers and flowers hung
from its windows; and with a great cry of 'Love and Peace Around
the World' the tram set off on this historic inaugural journey.

The first problem occurred at Blackpool city limits where the
tram lines stopped. This unforseen eventuality demanded the kind
of imaginative solution that only 'Fizzing' Sid could come up with.

'O.K. everybody,' he announced, thinking laterally, 'that's the end
of the ride. You can walk home the lot of you and none of you are
getting your fucking money back.'

It is in that spirit of greed and exploitation that Captain Magic's
Exploding Trouser buses have gone from strength to strength. Sid,
an older, richer man, now runs a fleet of buses equipped with every
luxury demanded by the new sophisticated breed of international
traveller. Some of the buses even have seats.

It was, therefore, in a mood of some excitement that I boarded
Sid's Trans-Asia Express and looked at the route map carefully
provided in the traveller's pack, which also contained my food for the
trip – a Tic-Tac and a packet of Nuttall's Mintoes. From London
we would drive to Dover, cross the Channel, then on to Paris,
down to Spain, over to Gibraltar, across the straits to Tangier,
through Morocco, Algeria, Libya, Egypt, Israel, Syria, Iraq, Iran,

Afghanistan, the USSR, China and finally down to Hanoi in Vietnam.

Just as the bus started Mr Fawncroft, a soup salesman from Parsons Green, pointed out to our tour guide, affectionately known as 'Mad Janet', that, owing to political problems, some of these countries might not let us in.

Mad Janet laughed away Mr Fawncroft's fears and said, 'Well we'll just have to cross that bim when we come to it, won't we?'

Mr Fawncroft asked her what a bim was, but Mad Janet merely pointed at the sky and smiled enigmatically. 'There's those who don't know their own mother when she's partial to "Celebrity Squares",' she averred.

The bus set off. Then it broke down. The AA was called and they took away two or three heavy drinkers. This loss of weight enabled the bus to start again. Then it stopped suddenly and then just as suddenly it started. Then it stopped a little less suddenly and we all had to transfer to another bus. We disembarked and embarked by which time they'd got the first bus started again and that went off to Dover saying we should catch it up if the second bus ever got started.

Mad Janet started whooing like an owl.

We finally got to Dover three months behind schedule, but luckily so was the boat.

It was a rough crossing. Mr Fawncroft said he'd crossed the Channel many times before and never known one quite as rough. Like the two seasoned travellers we were, we passed the time exchanging interesting anecdotes about our respective travel experiences. He told me about the time he nearly missed his turning on the B5209 and I told him about the time I nearly went to sleep and missed my stop on the Bakerloo line.

Meanwhile the sea churned and spumed so that periodically we were sick in each other's breast pockets. Thus our friendship was bonded.

We arrived in Paris at dawn. Paris has changed: Les Halles is now an indoor shopping complex; Montmartre is a tourist trap; Jean Cocteau is dead; and a sombrero is a large hat.

And yet the spirit of Paris shouts at one from every cobble, every stone, every hoarding, every electrical shop: '*Je suis Paris*,' it says. '*Qui le fuck êtes-vous?*'

Paris is a city of fine cuisine. Les Halles was once a huge open market, *le ventre de Paris*. And at 5.30 on a bleak spring morning it is still haunted by the ghosts of the old '*salmonellistes*' who once whistled cheerful Jacques Brel tunes as they unloaded the '*camions d'Enterovioform*'.

Paris is a city of café society. The Café des Ineptitudes is still there on the rue Cahiers du Cinéma. Here it was that Hemingway, Scott Fitzgerald, Gertrude Stein and the young Frank Bough were initiated into the secrets of Rugby League by Eddie Waring. Here it was, too, that Les Six, the legendary group of Parisian experimental composers, used to meet – Poulenc, Satie, Honegger, Sleepy, Grumpy and Dopey.

Paris a city of revolution. 1789, 1848, 1871, 1968 – the price of a *croque monsieur* and a bottle of Heineken goes up all the time and it is rumoured that, if it goes up to the full 2000, the cobbles will again be

A SILLY MAP OF PARIS

MONTMARTRE

prised from the streets and the barricades erected on the Avenue Hiroshima Mon Amour. As Voltaire, the inventor of electricity, puts it: '*L'État, c'est un cinéma à Kilburn*'.

Paris is a city of artists. Manet's *atelier* in the Boulevard Piff-Paff Nim is now open to the public and here one can learn much about the master's techniques. Rarely, for instance, did he draw things out of his head. Most of his best works were copied out of magazines. He invariably used a ruler for straight lines and often a rubber to rub out mistakes, sometimes even going so far as to turn over and start again. Many critics who have praised Manet's brushwork would be amazed to discover that he rarely even bothered to wash them, either letting them go dry and hard, or leaving them standing up in a jar so the bristles got all bent. In fact he didn't look after his things at all. Not like that nice Degas. You could eat your dinner off *his* paintbox, you really could, and the inside of his bathroom cabinet was a joy to the eye – so neat.

But, for the writer, Paris is, above all, a city of stationery shops. Rymaines in the Place Ya Ya Twiste is the second largest retail stationery outlet in Western Europe with an unrivalled selection of both box and ring files. Here writers from all over the world come to admire the very date stamp pads that Sartre used to buy; the same handsomely packaged notelets that Rimbaud would use when he was invited to a birthday party; even the paper-clip tidies that Antoine de St Exupéry tested to a height of 33,000 feet.

Voyages Bugaboo Frères: Service D'Autoroute – Paris à Soixante-le-Sayle.

I am riding on this French coach, heading towards the small village of Soixante-le-Sayle because I have developed a sudden interest in researching my family tree. Curiously enough this interest came about due to alternative medicine.

While we superciliously deride the Victorians for their blind faith in the promises of dubious pills, elixirs and potions, our generation blithely puts the same blind faith in any quackery calling itself 'alternative medicine'. Perfectly rational people are convinced that asthma can be cured by having knitting needles stuck up their arse or that strokes can be avoided by eating bees while having their bones broken by some untrained sadist who advertises in *Time Out* or the *Yellow Pages*. I admit to being a sucker for New Wave medicine myself and for some time I visited a Hypno-osteoacupuncturist whose ad I saw in an old copy of *Classic Car* magazine. At fifty quid a time, over the years, she managed to transform a small ache into a full-blown deformity. The only consolation was that I qualified for a free bus pass and an orange sticker for my car so I could park it in the food hall of Selfridges.

A WIERD DRAWING TO FILL UP SOME SPACE...

By Alexei Sayle. 1986.

However, several times while under the hypnotism part of my treatment I began to regress towards earlier incarnations. Suddenly I would speak in the voice of a dead uncle of mine – Albert Sayle, who fought in the Spanish Civil War. He commanded a company of Surrealists who during that bloody conflict mostly kept their artillery trained on a platoon of watches commanded by a watermelon. At other times I would shout about having Marmite rubbed into my trousers by a beautiful . . . but that's another story.

However, these experiences gave me the urge to travel the world seeking out my ancestors. So far through my researches I have found links with many famous relatives. For example QUEEN FATICEA (320 AD), legendary Queen of the Britons.

~Queen Faticea~

RED JAKE SAYLE 'Scourge of the Seven Seas' (1711–1756), a notorious pirate who had a thing about ginseng. He thought the stuff was a fraud and was of the opinion that people who sold it should be keel-hauled – hence his *soubriquet*. He was eventually hanged under the Trade Descriptions Act.

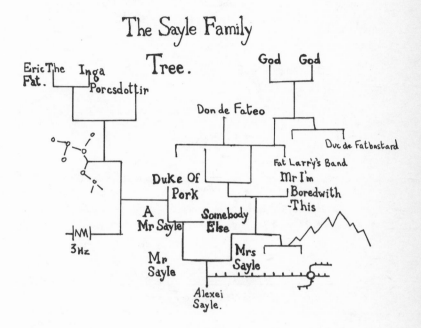

THE MARQUIS DE SAYLE , poet, writer, artist, madman. His name has become a synonym for immense sartorial cruelty. Amongst other excesses, he would use hot irons on his trousers, lock away his hat-boxes for months on end and falsely tell his underpants that they had won on the *Daily Mirror* Bingo.

ROY (SPRINGHEELS) SAYLE (1952–   ), captain and centre-forward for Pilchester Rovers, otherwise known as 'The Masked Player' because of the cunningly crafted mask he wears on the pitch in his lifelong bid to keep his true identity a secret. He has been capped

148 times and his dentist has just bought a second Porsche. Loved, respected and admired by everyone inside the game and out, amongst his other achievements: in 1958 he scored the winning goal in the FA Cup with two broken legs; in 1964, in a needle match against Belford Rangers, he took a hat-trick with a single throw-in; in the 1966 World Cup he won three-nil against Brazil – single-handed; and in 1983 he released a record called 'Ello John, Gotta New Motor' – oh shit, there goes my anonymity.

INIGO SAYLE (1683–1752), architect and builder. Specialised in cathedrals, palaces and loft conversions. He was made a saint for his work by Pope Alexei IX (See Below).

POPE ALEXEI IX (SEE BELOW) (1714–1748): the *soubriquet* 'See Below' was a result of Cardinal Lex (as he was known before he ascended to the Papacy) being a little absent-minded in the fly button department. Pope Alexei IX (See Below) won the Papacy in a game of Pick-a-Sticks with the College of Cardinals. His many pronouncements included *De Flegmaticus Orangjeboom* which made spitting at Dutch people a venial rather than a mortal sin. He was also the first Pope to wear ox-blood loafers with argyll socks.

LIM PIN SAYLE (623–692) Chinese poet. Most of his poems are untranslatable; e.g.:

> Fish in pond
> Lilies on side of pond
> Chicken in basket
> Flipping heck!

See what I mean? Either untranslatable or just plain bloody stupid. One or the other. He also wrote the small print on the six-year anti-corrosion guarantee for the Fiat Uno.

MAD BONK NICE BONK HERRING SAYLE (1251–1257). There was never really anybody called this. It's just that when you're inventing ancestors sometimes your brain goes loop-de-loop.

JUMBLE SAYLE. Ha ha ha bloody ha. That's what my friends used to call me at school. Or rather they would have done if I'd had any friends. In my dreams I used to have lots of friends who would call me such names as 'Jumble' in an affectionately mocking way. The reality was somewhat different. But then reality is always different from dreams. Mr Lewis says so. Personally I disagree with him but Mr Lewis says it's best if I don't disagree with him about things like that, otherwise he'll have to start writing down everything I say again and he won't let me carry on with the Community Reintegration Programme. Actually, if the truth be known, I'd rather not carry on with the Community Reintegration Programme. Cleaning out canals isn't my cup of tea. A cup of tea is more my cup of tea . . . as long as it's milky, with lots of sugar. That's my cup of tea. Jesus, I'm pissed again.

Dieting to Destruction.

The only way to lose weight is to eat less and do more. I should know – I've been on more diets than I've had hot dinners. One of the best was a high-fibre diet I went on; actually it was a chipboard diet – every day I used to eat two flat pack wardrobes and a self-assembly coffee table. I didn't do my shopping at Asda, I went to MFI instead. Another great diet I was on for a while was 'The Hollywood Dead Diet' – in this diet you achieve spectacular rapid weight loss by killing yourself – pretty soon you are down to the weight of a single atom.

One time I went on a very effective weight-loss programme. The only trouble was all the weight went from one place – my feet! I went from a size ten to a nine or eight or five. Pretty soon I was buying my shoes in Mothercare. I looked like a hot air balloon – a huge bulk tapering to a point at the bottom. In desperation I started eating my previous large amounts. For a while I was worried that the fat might come back in a totally new place – my nose, perhaps, or my thumbs. However, luckily the weight went back onto my feet and the story has a happy ending because with all the spare shoes I had left over I started a cut-price shoe store in Northamptonshire and became a millionaire.

POLL RESULTS

It's here at last. The results of this year's 'Great Bus Journeys' Readers' poll. There've been some surprises, some shocks, some sadness but a great response! So here's the results:

FAVOURITE LONDON CAKE SHOP
1. Coombes Lite Bite Cake Shop, Lillie Road, SW6.
2. Rolando's Patisserie, Tavistock Place, WC1
3. Grodzinski's, Goodge Street, W1

Up from last year's 94th place for Coombe's Lite Bite in SW6 but the previous number one – the Ancient Temple of Ankor Wat in Cambodia – drops to number six.

FAVOURITE CAKE
1. Rock Bun
2. Toasted Bun
3. Belgian Bun
4. Battenberg (slice)
5. King Hussein of Jordan

FAVOURITE CAKESTAND
1. Aspreys 'Mr Cake' Silver Upright.
2. Harvey Nichols Teak Folding Cakestand.
3. 'Just Cakestands' plc Neil Kinnock-shaped teacake holder.

FAVOURITE COMEDIAN
1. King Hussein of Jordan
2. Sooty
3. Alexei Sayle

34

From France I journeyed by bus and ferry to the Spanish province of the Canary Islands in order to catch some much needed winter sun. But although I returned with a golden tan I also returned with a vague and oppressive feeling of giddy uneasiness. This uneasiness is connected with topless beaches. As on beaches all over Europe, many of the women in Lanzarote sunbathed topless – which is of course nobody's business but theirs. However my reaction to this toplessness is more of a mess. The accepted cliché about nudity is that after a few minutes it becomes irrelevant, but is this true? After all men are constantly being bombarded with photographs of the naked top halves of women. These photos are used to sell things – car spares, Sunday newspapers, aftershave. When suddenly you are surrounded by the naked top halves of women in the flesh is it possible to switch off and not ogle?

After a couple of days lounging on the beach I felt as if somebody kept pointing a double-barrelled shotgun at my head. After a week I was dizzy, disorientated and ill. I felt so bad I went to see the local doctor and he diagnosed my illness as a bad case of topless overdose. He said it was not so much a case of sun-stroke, more like what you might call a bad case of breast-stroke.

I was forced to get the plane back to Britain and I was further unsettled by the disturbing and weird things that happened to my holiday purchases.

Have you noticed how the nice quiet leather jacket or the sensible fashionable shoes which you bought in the street market while on holiday have somehow totally transmogrified? When you get your vacation purchases home and unpack them, the nice jacket has suddenly sprouted hideous giant lapels, has shrunk about five sizes, and has grown gruesome funny buttons and a multitude of pleats, pouches, loops and buckles. The nice tasteful shoes you bought turn out to be pink winkle-pickers with eight-inch cuban heels and gold tips on the toes, and the trousers you purchased make you look like Coco the Clown.

Is this change something to do with the unpressurised air in plane cargo holds or perhaps something to do with the material suitcases are made out of? We must be told now!

It's good to see that package tours are finally being offered to Europe's last inaccessible country, Albania. Albania, a rigid Marxist–Leninist Balkan state, has, after remaining a fortress since the war, started to welcome visitors. Having been a Marxist–Leninist myself, I have already had experience of Albania. Round about 1978 I went on a delegation to this Adriatic workers' paradise. All went well until one night our hosts gave a recital of Albanian revolutionary songs. Then they turned to us and said 'Now you sing us some of your English revolutionary songs'.

Now, unlike most countries, we do not have a history of popular revolutionary songs. George Formby never sang 'I Will Bring About the Proletarian Millenium with My Little Stick of Blackpool Rock' and 'On Ilkley Moor Baht 'At' hardly fits the bill.

So after a couple of minutes of silence I jumped up and sang two verses of the Sex Pistols' 'Anarchy in the UK' and then spat on a member of the Central Committee. I got out of prison three years later.

MARCH

Yesterday I was having a few cocktails at the Commonwealth Institute with some intellectual friends and we all agreed what an underrated and interesting place Acton is. In order to rectify this situation we present . . .

The 'Great Bus Journeys' Round Acton Sight-Seeing Trip.

The bus leaves from Strumpenny Gardens, Acton, at 0900 hours every Thursday. Passengers should wear pacamacs, carry pale green lunch boxes containing hard boiled eggs and oranges and try to spend as much of the day as possible worrying in case they forgot to unplug the hoover.

FIRST STOP
98 Strumpenny Gardens, once the home of Jack Flinch, the celebrated eighteenth-century horse thief. When the authorities raided Jack's home on July 25, 1782 they discovered sixty horses wedged up his chimney. In his defence Jack claimed that he was liberating the horses from the slavery of life between the shafts of drapers' vans and teaching them a decent trade.

'If a child can go up a chimney, why not a horse?' he demanded. London's fashionable society took up his cry and, before long, no soirée was complete without a handsome bay or an elegant chestnut neighing in the up draught.

But the judge was not inclined to clemency and Jack was publicly hanged at Tyburn. Owing to an administrative oversight all sixty horses were hanged with him. A fine sight they made too. The house is now the National Museum of Various Things and contains a fine collection of Lion Brand airmail envelopes.

From Strumpenny Gardens we turn left into Main Lane.

SECOND STOP
42 Main Lane, once the home of the famous clairvoyant Madame Sikorsky, who gained a wide following in the 1890s. Many great people flocked to her for guidance and enlightenment, including Oscar Wilde and his brother Marty; Frank Harris, his brother 'Bomber' and his sister Anita; Henry James and the rest of the James Gang; and Tin-Tin with his dog Rin. All were much impressed.

Madame Sikorsky claimed she received 'messages' from 'the other world' *via* her spirit guide, a Red Indian Chief by the name of Bloxo, which included a number of predictions of future events. Unfortunately these were all in a defunct dialect of Cherokee but, for the record, in 1989 there should be a 'Fnim tum num b'yar s'nuth'. Madame Sikorsky was later unmasked as a fraud and Bloxo was revealed to be a very much alive Norwegian seaman named Big Honk Hammerdong.

We proceed down Main Lane . . .

Good. He's just gone to the lav to be sick. I've just got time to slip this in. . . . This is David Stafford here, you can see my name at the top of the column in letters that get smaller and smaller every week. You must help me! That fat bastard Alexei is holding me hostage. Like that letter said the other week I write all the funny stuff. He just does the stupid drawings. 'I think I'll draw a pig wearing some fucking trousers,' he said before. 'The fucking readers won't know if it's fucking funny or not.' And he tells lies all the time. He doesn't drink in the Commonwealth Institute – he's been barred from there. He goes to an afternoon drinking club called the Rigor Mortis. He's been there today, that's why he's sick. He only ever eats Cornish pasties and baked beans and wanders about in his underpants and he doesn't pay me anything at all. Please help me! I'm . . .

THIRD STOP

The largest building on Main Lane is the First Church of the Boisterously Sceptical. The church was built in 1903. The architect was F. Stanwyck Blissel. The pews were made at the Wolverhampton Pew Works and designed by Herbert Livingholme. The font was carved by Diana Quick. The stained glass window was constructed by Anna Cropper and Martin Shaw. Other parts were played by Trader Faulkner and members of the BBC Repertory Company.

More interesting than the church building is the theology of Boisterous Scepticism, a taste of which is given by this extract from its creed:

> PRIEST: I believe in God the Father Almighty.
> CONGREGATION (*chant*): Wanker. Wanker. Wanker.
> PRIEST: Maker of heaven and earth.
> CONGREGATION: That's not what it said on *Horizon*.
> PRIEST: And in Jesus Christ his only Son our Lord.
> CONGREGATION: (*Whistle a short extract from the 'Colonel Bogey' march*).
> PRIEST: Who was conceived by the Holy Ghost.
> CONGREGATION: Here we go, here we go, here we go . . .
> PRIEST: Born of the Virgin Mary.
> CONGREGATION: Tell it to the marines, pull the other one it's got bells on, do me a favour . . . etc.

FOURTH STOP

Lunch at the Acton Recreation Ground 'Fancy Pants' McCaulay Memorial Tea Rooms. Diners might like to observe, preserved under glass, the actual trousers which Mr McCaulay wore. By modern standards they cannot be considered particularly fancy.

FIFTH STOP

Free time to relax in the sunshine and enjoy the smell of dogshit on the extensive lawns of Acton Recreation Grounds. Sometimes in the Recreation Grounds several big men can be seen beating the shit out of a moustachioed gent who pretends he's a writer and TV presenter

A PIG WEARING
SOME TROUSERS.

called David Something or other. The big men shout, 'Don't fuck
with the column! Don't fuck with the column!'

At 1500 hours we board the bus once again and make our way to:

SIXTH STOP
43 Ronchester Place, once the home of the notorious master spy
Ron Jenkins. Jenkins was at Oxford in the '30s working as a riveter at
the Morris motor factory in Cowley. He came under the influence of
Burgess and Maclean, helped Maclean develop his famous tooth-
paste and was thus recruited as a double agent into the KGB.

After the war he became junior woodwork teacher at the Dixie
Dean Grammar School in Acton. He was not ideally placed to pass
British secrets to his spy-masters, but he did his best. In 1961 he was
arrested when he was caught red-handed putting details of the
Fourth Form woodwork syllabus into a known dead letter box. He
was tried, found guilty, and sentenced to life imprisonment. Two
years later, after lengthy negotiations, he was swapped at Check-
point Charlie for a bag of balloons and a pencil.

Traffic allowing, the bus should return to Strumpenny Gardens
in time for a late tea of Cornish pasties and baked beans.

I am very fond of drinking. People often say to me 'Alexei, why are you drunk all the time?' I say 'Because I can afford to be!' Drinking never does me any harm. The only trouble is . . . the erm . . . the erm . . . the blackouts! – Do you ever have blackouts? You know, you have a few pints then suddenly everything goes black and you wake up next morning in an unfurnished flat in Brussels dressed as Santa Claus and a man comes through the door and says: 'Hello Mr Saunders. I've squashed all the turnips, should I bring the goat in now?' That happens to me all the time.

The reason I mention drinking is that there was a bit in the paper this week about how publicans should report people they suspect are drunk drivers. I agree with this completely. Drinking and driving is a despicable, cowardly act, where some immoral person, in pursuit of their own selfish pleasure, risks killing or maiming some innocent party. It is only perhaps in the countryside where there is absolutely no public transport and friends and pubs are scattered over a large area that drink-driving can be understood – if not excused. For the rural drunk I propose there should be designed a special Drinko-matic car. It would be made of soft foam rubber and would be powered by the motor from an electric carving knife so it could only go at 3 m.p.h. It would have a rotating light on top and light bulbs would flash on and off the word DRUNK. Thus the country alcoholics could very slowly wend their way home. Sober people would see them coming miles away and the drunk-driver could tumble into ditches or plough into bus queues without causing the usual massacre.

Things just get better and better for me. I've got another smashing new girlfriend. This one's also a model. She's a topless model – that means her head screws off.

PART 9

THE FURTHER ADVENTURES OF MICK AND HIS MIDGET POPE.

TO PROVE HIS MIRACULOUS POWERS MICK'S MIDGET POPE PRODUCED POUND COINS FROM MICK'S NOSE AND FILLED A PAUL MASSON CALIFORNIA CARAFE WITH THEM ON THE STAGE OF THE NATIONAL THEATRE.

AN APOLOGY

Owing to a misprint in last week's column, the impression may have been given that I am the proprietor of a pet shop in Bristol. Furthermore, many people may have been misled into believing that I am an expert on the ailments of eels.

I would like to publicly state that I have no connection, nor have I ever had any connection, with a Bristol pet shop and, while I do have a commonsense knowledge of eel ailments, due modesty would prevent me describing myself as an expert. Therefore, if you have any enquiries concerning eels please contact the British Eel Society, Slither House, Ealing, London W3.

When people meet me they are often deeply impressed with my calmness, my inner peace and my at one-ness with the world.

These people frequently ask me how I achieve this detachment from the pressures of the world. Well, the answer is that when I was in my mid-twenties I went to study with some very nice monks in Tibet. While I was with the monks I studied very hard. The very wise monks were able to coach me for an HND in Business Studies with a sandwich course option in Industrial Accountancy and Shorthand Typing. This now means that I am conversant with double-entry book-keeping, cash flow, and management strategy and, as a result, I am wise, successful and in tune with the world.

However, my calm inner peace means that I am not very outgoing in the usual brainless showbiz way. In fact you could describe me as a bit of an enigma – that's the word you could use to describe me – an enigma, a mysterious presence. I am not part of the bitchy showbiz world.

Sure, very occasionally, I may silently appear at some glittering party escorted by a beautiful companion of either sex, but then turn around a few seconds later and I have vanished.

Nobody knows where I live or what I do most of the time. I may be seen one day riding a powerful motorbike along the Corniche at Nice, the next day playing the oboe in the Thailand State Orchestra, you never know with me. I do not have many friends in the entertainment world, rather I have my own circle of friends – managers of medium-sized ice hockey teams, London Transport tour guides and the proprietors of Harrogate gift shops.

However, because I am an enigma, I have found weird stories tend to circulate about me, strange myths and urban legends surround me.

People are always saying to me 'Cor what about that time you ate that fire extinguisher!' or 'Blimey! Did you really walk through Television Centre with a lobster on a lead?' These stories are all untrue but, deny them as I might, they still spread.

Those who have worked with me will testify to my matchless professionalism, but the other thing is that people in show business start blaming me for the things I had nothing to do with. Lazy TV researchers say 'Oh I'm sorry I haven't done those scripts, Mr Director, but Alexei Sayle ran into my office and stuffed black forest gâteau into my typewriter!' or 'I'm sorry I haven't got those vital props, Ms Producer, but Alexei Sayle just burnt my house down!'

In some countries I have even achieved the status of a sort of bogey man. In Sweden for instance there's a nursery rhyme parents tell naughty children who won't go to sleep. It goes:

Teg tag volvo zig zed
Der man from der *Sunday Mirror* will chompen yor head!

There are times when I accuse the government of being a pack of corrupt greedy animals, or I say the ruling class have destroyed the country through senility and greed and should all be executed and people say I'm carping. This is completely untrue. I am not carping. Carp are in fact very happy-go-lucky stupid fish who will put up with almost anything. Haddock on the other hand are extremely bad-tempered fellows who boil at any injustice they may encounter, while swimming in the ocean deep. So when I say, for example, that judges

44

are senile old gits with the brain power of an early computer (they can only remember one and a half things at the same time: if they tell you the time they forget what their name is) then I am in no way carping. I am, in fact, haddocking.

London Regional Transport: A2 Airport Express –
Upper Woburn Place to Heathrow Airport.

Despite my denial last week that I had anything to do with a pet shop in Bristol or that I was an expert on eel ailments, I have still been inundated with letters asking for advice about pet eels. As I have said before I am unqualified to answer these enquiries. However, in case there are any eel specialists reading this, I am publishing some of these letters in full.

Dear Alexei,

I read in the *Daily Telegraph* the other day that an eel can suffocate if it breathes wrong. But what, in this context, is 'wrong'?

E. F., Kilburn.

Dear Mr Sayle,

My brother says that an eel is an unsuitable creature to keep in this country as a pet because of its innate dishonesty. I maintain that if you start out trusting an eel and bring it up in an atmosphere of trust, it will learn to be trustworthy. Which of us is right?

T. C. (age 12), Rickmansworth
P.S. I thought you were great in *OTT*.

Dear Fat Bastard,

My eel is afraid of gas. He whimpers every time he goes near
the meter. Could it be that this poor deluded creature thinks
he is a badger? His name is Gilbert, if it is of any relevance.
Actually his name isn't Gilbert, it is Hugh, but he is
embarrassed about it and prefers to be called Gilbert. I don't
know why he should be embarrassed about being called Hugh.
I named him after the late leader of the Labour Party, Hugh
Gaitskell.

I. I., Charlton

P.S. I saw you at a benefit concert last March. Could I have my
money back?

Dear Mr Sayle,

My eel called Miriam has the irritating habit of humming
quietly to herself. When I tell her to stop she says she wasn't
aware she was doing it and then, after a short pause, continues.
I'm sure she only does it because she knows it infuriates me so
much. Are eels spiteful?

L. G. (Mr), Hilversum.

P.S. My wife often gets you mixed up with Lenny Henry. I
must say there is an uncanny resemblance. Have other people
noticed this?

I was on my way to the airport for a quick visit to the United States,
where I am very famous. At one time this trip would have been
impossible, as I used to have a terrible phobia about flying.
    I acquired the aforementioned phobia skimming into Varna
Airport in Bulgaria. Ostensibly I was in Bulgaria with my parents for

46

a holiday at the Black Sea resort of Slumpny Dumpny (Golden Cod). I say 'ostensibly' because, as I am in a mood for confession, I may as well reveal that I am in fact the notorious 'Fifth Man'. This is the fact that the British government has been fighting to conceal.

I was recruited into the Russian Intelligence Service by Kim Philby in 1959 when I was aged seven, while I was at a North West Area meeting of the Woodcraft Folk (the paramilitary wing of the Co-op). For years the Politburo was kept informed of all the nicknames of the teachers at Anfield Road Junior School, the temper of the lollipop woman and the outrageous price of sherbert in Liverpool 4. Later, when I passed the eleven-plus, my greatest scoop was to inform my control accurately in advance of the likely 'O' level History questions.

However, I digress. There was something about the rudimentary construction of the Bulgarian Airlines Kerensky IL20 which gave me a terrible feeling of dread and fear of flying, which, until earlier this year, I have been unable to shake off. This is not to say that I haven't flown. I have to fly for my work. I have travelled by air to the United States, where I work frequently and am a big star, to Australia, Finland, Spain etc. But in order to fly I would have to take a cocktail of drugs – a mixture of a tranquillizer, usually Ativan, and a drug called Propananol, commonly known as Beta-blockers.

Taking these drugs meant that I could fly, or indeed sky-dive if I wanted to, but there could be side-effects. Having overdosed rather on a flight from Australia I terrorised an entire Jumbo jet first by sitting in my seat with my anorak hood backwards on my head and my headphones on top of the hood, yelling a song at the top of my voice; then by searching all over the plane for a small dog I was certain had been hidden somewhere aboard. Anybody who has seen me at an airport terminal draped over a luggage trolley and trundling it about on tiptoe, bonking into walls, will now know the reason why.

However, by and large, I was happy with this situation. It was only when I flew into Miami, Florida in January this year to make a film that things really started to go wrong. One of the problems with tranquillizers is that it is difficult to know when they have been flushed out of the system. I would often come to in an important meeting or on location halfway up a mountain without the slightest

47

idea what I'd been up to minutes before. (Although others who'd been present at these blackouts always seemed at pains to keep carrots out of my way.)

The day after my arrival in Murder City, USA, in January, I took a walk into town passing through the largely black-populated Flagler Street district, fairly safe during the day but extremely dangerous at night. Suddenly I developed this terrible urge to imitate the street people I was passing. 'Yo dude! How's ya momma?' I started shouting, talking and walking in bad imitation of one of Kool and the Gang. 'Wass happenin, Jim? Ya mofo man! Solid! Solid, ma man, jest solid!' I squawked before my wife bundled me into a taxi and drove ma ass at high speed outta dere.

From this euphoria I was plunged into terrible gloom, although whether this was the drugs or Miami, which is the most awful place in the world, it's hard to say. After returning to England and eight weeks of jet-lag I resolved – no more pills. But how was I to fly?

I finally opted to try hypnotism. Every week I would go to see this man in Wimpole Street. I'd sit in an old-fashioned armchair covered in doilies, he'd count from one to ten, I'd close my eyes and we'd be off.

After doing various relaxation exercises I would then be told to imagine that I was in a plane flying happily along. To enhance the effect the hypnotist used a couple of cheap 'Boots' brand tape recorders to provide sound effects. When I was imagining myself in the departure lounge he would play the noise of crowds and the clank of luggage trolleys, when the imaginary plane was taking off he would provide the noise of screaming jet engines and so on. We travelled all over the world in my mind. Every week my friends would ask which country I'd been to and then complain that I hadn't bought them any duty-free.

The only problem was that the eminent hypnotist would some-times get his tapes mixed up so that while I was imagining as hard as I could that I was over the Bay of Biscay tucking into Shrimps Montego he would suddenly play the sound effects tape for Terminal Three of Heathrow. Suddenly my imaginary plane would be flooded with the sound of bing-bong announcements and arguing families. This caused me great confusion – flying but not flying, on

48

the ground but not on the ground, in Wimpole Street but not in Wimpole Street.

The strange thing is it worked. I now fly everywhere, in fact in order to achieve the serenity I now feel while flying I fly to places it is completely pointless to fly to. I bet you've never heard of Birkenhead's Hatton International Airport, or Derby Intercontinental – Terminal Six. But I've been there. I may have to take to hypnotism again to stop flying.

London Regional Transport: Route 113 – Edgware Station to Oxford Circus via Mill Hill.

EELS – ANOTHER APOLOGY

In last week's column a number of letters appeared from people wanting advice on the best ways to keep eels as pets. The reaction to these letters has been huge and horrifying. I publish one example typical of the thousands of letters received.

Dear Sir,

I am literally shocked, nay horrified, nay literally shocked, to discover that in this so-called enlightened twentieth-century civilised society we live in, the practise of eel-keeping is still alive and wriggling.

It has been proven by West German scientists that, as far as intelligence goes, eels rank just below dolphins, just above Ralph McTell and miles above Shakin' Stevens. And yet these intelligent creatures are literally trapped and bought and sold in the market place as though they were cattle! This traffic is, of course, literally illegal.

An eel kept in a cage suffers severe stress and trauma. This has been frequently observed by scientists in both West Germany and in America. Caged eels refuse to eat or sleep,

49

they cease cleaning their beaks or feathers – eventually the feathers literally fall out – they do not sing or perform normal nesting or breeding functions. Furthermore . . .

Eagles! Sorry, I meant eagles, not eels. I take it all back. I'm sorry.
Literally,
V.M. (Hotel California, Paddington)

As I passed the Café Royal I recalled the famous Brown Stain on the Wall, which bears testament to the time in 1910 when the playwright T. Harrison Hibble-Nibblick attacked the critic Pawkesly Mawksley with a large custard for calling his play *Mr Tomkinson's Trousers* 'a wiggly bit of fish placed in the shoes of the public' in his column in the *London Chronicle*. Those were the days, the artistic community was awash and constantly enlivened by feuds, grudges, calculated insults and public scandals. Artists would constantly be 'cutting dead' other artists in the Strand, often stepping under horse-drawn omnibuses rather than share the same stretch of pavement. One recalls Beau Brummel's famous insult to the Prince Regent – 'Fuck me you're a bit of a fucking porker, ain't ya?' And of course in the '20s rival Surrealists were constantly fighting duels on Hampstead Heath over some imagined insult, although as their weapons were alarm clocks at two hundred paces the event was often tedious and inconclusive.

But these days people (certainly in my business) are too chicken-shit and afraid to bear a grudge. I go round constantly spreading bile, invective and insults. I'm not talking to people I've never met. I'm having artistic feuds with people in Belgium who don't know I exist. But it's no good – everybody, all the people I insult, are still kissy-kissy, darling how lovely to see you, when we meet.

So in a last vain attempt to get a feud going I'm going to insult you. YES, YOU reading this. YOU! You know I think you're a farty-faced, pig-bummed, hatrack-headed piece of lethal asbestos. I do honest. I think you're crap. And another thing, for the past six years I've been fucking your Husband/Wife/Girlfriend/Boyfriend/Dog/Cat/Parrot/Gas Cooker* and they think you're crap too. And also your favourite Coat/Pullover/Pair of Trousers/Jacket/Hat* that you wear all the time – I think it makes you look like an aubergine. So there. And all your friends are crap and your House/Flat/Caravan/Cardboard Box/Sewer* where you live is crap. And everything you think, say, spit out and sit on is crap.

All the best,
Alexei Sayle
PS   See you for a drink on Tuesday, as usual.

Today is an important day for me. I have finally achieved a lifetime's ambition. After years of hard work, toil and endeavour, I now have more money than sense.

More girlfriend trouble for me. I met this really smashing girl at a party, we got talking and I thought it was great when she told me that she was from the Isle of Wight, somewhere I've never been.

But then I was stunned when she told me she was from Cowes!

There I go again, getting off with a girl who's got weird parents!

*Delete where inappropriate.

A GREAT BUS JOURNEYS SPECIAL OFFER
LEARN THE GUITAR IN SECONDS!

WHAT DID YOU SAY?

I said: **'LEARN THE GUITAR IN SECONDS!!!'**

WHY WOULD I WANT TO DO THAT?

FOR THESE REASONS:

Ever wished you could be the life and soul of your local wine bar or tube station?

Ever wanted to be very rich and have cassettes of your music played in sales reps' Vauxhall Cavaliers on every major motorway in the country?

Ever wanted to be more DYNAMIC, more PURPOSEFUL, more SEXUALLY PERSUASIVE?

YES, OF COURSE I HAVE, BUT HOW CAN I ACHIEVE THESE WONDERFUL THINGS?

A unique Great Bus Journeys/Alexei Sayle offer can bring you all this and more.

How often have you said to yourself: 'I wish I could play a musical instrument?'

EVER SUCH A LOT.

Well now you CAN!!!

HOW?

Easy. Send off the clip coupon from this page of *Great Bus Journeys of the World* together with the front covers of any four other Methuen Books purchased over the last six months, complete the slogan 'I think Alexei Sayle is fab because he has an enormous p---s' and we will send you absolutely free (ecx. P&P) the Alexei Sayle 'Knopfler' model push-button guitarette (illustrated actual size).

YES, BUT WHEN I'VE GOT IT, HOW DO I PLAY IT?

SIMPLE! Just wrap a tea towel round your head, press the buttons and off you go.

**Button One plays all the solos from 'Brothers in Arms'.

**Button One plays all the solos from 'Love Over Gold'.

**Button One plays all the other Mark Knopfler solos.

**None of the other buttons do fuck all.

ARE THERE ANY OTHER ADVANTAGES?

YES!!

**No messy practising.
**No rivets, glue or staples required.
**Will work to a depth of 200 feet.
**No batteries required.

AND WILL I REALLY BE ABLE TO PLAY IN SECONDS?

YES!!!!!!!

FANCY A DRINK?

O.K.

APRIL

As the bus pulls off the motorway and noses towards Birmingham centre I again experience the familiar stab of terror. Something has happened here.

It started out well enough in the winter of 1981/82. I was offered my first regular slot on a new, live, late-night TV programme – way ahead of the rest of the Comic Strip crew, I was headed for Teeveeland.

The name of the show was (spooky music, a terrified scream echoes in an empty building) 'O . . . T . . . T'.

At first things seemed fine. Sure, some of the sketch material was feeble. But I was good, Lenny Henry was good, the show was packed with vibrant life. Looking back it was certainly more genuinely live and subversive than the cardboard middle-class 'anarchy' of subsequent shows. It was genuinely regional – it was happy to come from Birmingham and wasn't tainted with supercilious Londoniswhereitsatism. (One of the irritating aspects of the Edinburgh Festival is to see the young comedians all doing their funny routine about Hampstead Theatre Club or *Time Out* or the funny shops in the Holloway Road or the buskers in Covent Garden, which work in London only on a cheap laugh of recognition, to an audience of bemused Scots.) It was multi-racial, both in front of and behind the camera. Perhaps best of all it lacked the awful improving didacticism of most television. It didn't try and patronisingly improve the viewer in any way, it was just a load of people behaving badly in front of the camera. It was also enormously popular – between seven and eight million viewers made it the most popular show ever at that time of night.

And yet, and yet, every week bright and early on a Monday morning the producer would be hauled into his bosses' office for the most terrible bollocking. Why? The answer was – letters. Letters. People in power – TV executives, and the like – pay a ridiculous and inordinate amount of attention to those who 'write in'. These executives reckon that if a hundred people write letters complaining about a show, they represent the views of many thousands more. A show can be made or broken by letters. And yet, of course, the truth is that people who 'write in' are not representative at all – they are fucking nut-cases. 'Writing in' is one of the things normal ordinary people just do not do – they may think about it from time to time but the letter never gets posted. Nevertheless people in power – TV executives and the editors of London listings magazines – are convinced that they are the most important barometers of popularity.

That is why I have a confession to make. When my column first appeared in *Time Out* it was greeted with universal indifference by the public so, knowing the importance of letters, I started 'writing in'. Using many aliases, different hand-writing, stationery and typewriters, so as not to alert the editor, I took the bus all over London posting the letters. At first I sent in many letters praising the column, saying how great and fantastic it was. Then, in case anyone got suspicious, I started throwing in the odd letter slagging it off and saying how crap it was – every letter that has ever been printed about my column has been written by me; every letter that will be 'written in' in the future will be written by me. I also wrote most of the letters about Julie Burchill. I also wrote a letter to the *Daily Mail* about slugs, but they didn't print that.

I've got another new girlfriend. She's called Angela Peabody. She's really great-looking. She's very sweet, small, green and round.

Now at last the truth can be told in this scoop 'Great Bus Journeys' exclusive. I can for the first time reveal that I, me, am the greatest supergrass in the history of British crime!

I am known as the scourge of the underworld because I, probably, have given the grateful police details of almost every crime committed in the last ten years. For example, it was me myself who told the boys in blue every last detail – names, cars used, hiding places – of the Great Train Robbery. I told them last Wednesday. Also during the week that big shipment of cocaine that was hidden in the rusty container arrived. As soon as I read about it in the paper I rushed straight round to Scotland Yard and told them all about it.

Not only do I help our own cops but approximately three years ago it gave me great satisfaction to be able to tell the Boston Police force that the infamous Boston Strangler was in fact one Albert de Salvo.

Until revealing this scoop exclusive I have, for obvious reasons, had to keep the fact that I was a supergrass very quiet. The reason I can now speak is because (as you probably know) if you give the bobbies top grade inside criminal info like me, then they give you loads of money, a new home and, most important, a new identity so that underworld figures can't bump you off.

I had a bit of trouble with the police Supergrass Squad over my new identity because the new identity I wanted was that of Desmond Lynam, the moustachioed man who presents *Grandstand* and *Midweek Sports Special* on BBC1. I really wanted to be him. He seemed such a nice calm man. I'm sure he's got a nice house and a nice family and I bet he's a hoot at after-dinner speaking and I bet he's matey with Emlyn Hughes and even the Saint and Greavsie, even though they work for ITV.

So anyway the law finally fixed it so I could be Desmond, which means I'll be presenting *Grandstand* on Saturday – see if you can spot the difference.

Incidentally, a sad man called Reg from Doncaster got my identity.

THE UNITED STATES

Miami City Bus Lines: Route 51 – Coral Gables Terminal to Flagler Street and Secundo Avenue via Biscayne Boulevard.

Letter from a Fat Bastard in America

'What is Alexei doing in America?' you ask. 'Has he been snapped up at last by Hollywood?' Well, no. It all started when I bought a step-ladder in the Northampton branch of Do It All. Buying a step-ladder entitled me to enter a competition offering me 'The Holiday of my Dreams'.

To me this sounded a very odd promise. In the holiday of my dreams I would wake up in a Mediterranean villa, walk outside and dive into the pool. But the pool would be full of little kittens instead of water and all the little kittens would have the faces of television newsreaders and then the one that looked like Gordon Honeycombe would turn round and say with great significance, 'Watch out for the pedal bins, Mr so-called Farthingay!' and I would be very worried because I don't know what this means, so I would try to run away but the ground has gone all sort of sludgy and I find that I can't move my feet and the kitten/newsreaders (except they're not kittens or newsreaders any more but people who look like the audience on *Top of the Pops*) they don't seem to have any difficulty walking through sludge at all and then it all changes and I'm at this sort of party and all my primary school teachers are there telling me to button my lip, only I can't because the button's come off.

In fact Miami is much worse than that. The amount of advertising on TV, radio and all other media is enormous, plus of course, there is a tremendous amount of 'sponsorship'. For instance in America this column would probably have to demean itself by changing its name to the Alexei Sayle/Pedigree Chum Column. Thank God things aren't so bad in Britain.

However, being abroad can give one a better perspective on some things at home and so this week I would like to make a few frank, fearless, unprejudiced comments about London's transport policy in general and ask this question: what do the planners think they're playing at when they site bus stops in the most useless places?

Why do people travel on buses? To get to their place of work of course, but also to get to leisure facilities and shops. Which shops in particular? Obviously the shops that offer the best range of goods at unbeatable prices. And in this day and age you can't really talk about unbeatable prices without talking about RUMBELOWS. Braun hairstyling kits for as little as £9.99! Need I say more?

In a recent survey it was discovered that a staggering 97.3 per cent of bus stops within the London Transport area are more than a staggering three hundred yards from a branch of RUMBELOWS. And yet another survey revealed that a staggering 94.6 per cent of Londoners travelling by bus declared that the main purpose of their journey was to take advantage of RUMBELOWS staggering price savers.* Staggered? I am.

What mindlessness can dictate such an inhuman policy? The very idea of forcing an unwitting populace to walk three hundred yards or more to purchase an Aiwa personal stereo for as little as £49.99 reeks of the worst excesses of fourteenth-century Sweden. So here is my message to the transport planners: get your act together! London will not be a safe place to live until all London buses have one destination and one destination only: RUMBELOWS where the price is always right.

Anyway, I am not one of those stars who only travels by flash limousine and only goes to superstar parties. I think it is vitally important for me to walk the streets and go to ordinary pubs – I am so dedicated I try to get to sixteen or seventeen different pubs every night.

The only real problem that I ever encounter on my wanderings is that people are constantly mistaking me for the Australian film superstar Mel Gibson!

* Surveys conducted by LIARPLAN. Sample: 100 people on buses who were going to RUMBELOWS.

Wherever I go people compliment me on my performances in the *Mad Max* movies, or ask me what Tina Turner is really like. It's only when they look closely they realise it's me and not Mel – then there is much embarrassment.

I wouldn't normally mention this but the other day when I was getting out of my limousine on my way to a superstar launch party for the London Film Festival when who should I bump into but good old Mel Gibson!

Well, over a few lagers we got chatting and eventually Mel revealed that he has exactly the same problem as me! Wherever he goes in the world people shout at him 'Ello John! Gotta New Motor' or ask him if Rik Mayall is as zany and madcap as he appears, or try to get him to do bits of my routines.

In fact, once, he told me, he was trapped in a bar in Tennessee by some truckers and had to sing four verses of my song 'Didn't You Kill My Brother' (a big hit in the States) and perform my famous tattoo routine from *The Young Ones* because they didn't believe he wasn't me and wouldn't let him leave.

It's a funny old world really, isn't it?

While here in the States I thought I'd met this great new girlfriend – then she told me she was from Buffalo! Why, oh why, can't I meet a girl with normal parents?

Greyhound Bus Lines: Route 28 – New York to LA.

Somewhere in the deep south events started to go bad for me. I lost my last cent in a game of craps (a disgusting and messy game, if you ask me). I was busted flat in Baton Rouge when I met Bobby McGee – a sanitary engineer from Maltby, Yorkshire. Together me and Bobby McGee decided to hitch to LA.

At the Interstate a big eighteen-wheeler riding from Billious, Connecticut clear across to Bad Smell, Oregon, with a shipment of hairdressing requisites stopped and we climbed aboard. The truck driver was an old-timer who used to drive the Baltimore to Utah run way back in the bad old days before they had trucks.

'Used to do it in my bare feet!' he said. Then he gave a hissing laugh and cussed some. Then he sang one of the old time trucking songs:

I've got eighteen wheels on the road
Pulling down this heavy load
Baltimore to that old Pacific Sea
And when the engine stops and I take some feed
When I drink my coffee, well I like to read,
And there's only one writer means anything to me.

Doris Lessing, Doris Lessing,
She's a writer who knows all there is about trucks.
And there surely ain't no messing
When it comes to Doris Lessing,
Well, next to her them other writers sucks.

Well I tell no lie, but I'm telling you
That my daddy was a trucker too
And just before he died he said, 'My son, take heed.
'Well I can't give you no advice
'About whiskey, women, cards or dice
'But when it comes to books there's only one to read.'

Doris Lessing, Doris Lessing,
She's a writer who knows all there is about trucks.
And there surely ain't no messing
When it comes to Doris Lessing,
Well, next to her them other writers sucks.

In a bar way down in Tonopah
Some bad guy really went too far,
Said he thought that Fay Weldon was real fine.
Like all other truck drivers' literary discussions
Well, this one ended in concussion
When I punched him clear across the county line.

Doris Lessing, Doris Lessing,
She's a writer who knows all there is about trucks.
And there surely ain't no messing
When it comes to Doris Lessing,
Well, next to her them other writers sucks.

The truck driver dropped us off in Oven Chips, Missouri.

New York to LA Part II.

The story so far: Me and Bobby McGee – a sanitary engineer from Maltby, Yorks – on a British Poundstretcher holiday are hitching across the States after being thrown off a Greyhound bus. A truck driver has dropped us off in Oven Chips, Missouri.

Now read on. . . .

Bobby approached a group of old-timers and asked if there was anywhere in town he could stay.

'Last strangers who came to town,' one said in a high-pitched nasal voice, 'stayed on the barn door. Leastways they stayed there until the nails rusted through. But then, they was Democrats.'

All the old-timers laughed and spat and cussed. Bobby and I shifted our weight from one foot to the other uncomfortably.

'Don't suppose you folks are Democrats now?' another of the old-timers asked, eyeing us suspiciously.

'No, we're not Democrats . . .' said Bobby, with a broad, beautiful smile, 'we're Communists.'

Fortunately, before they nailed us to the barn door, they asked us if we had any last requests. I requested that, before they killed us, they should all read Robert Tressel's *Ragged-Trousered Philanthropists*.

When they'd finished reading, as I expected, they were excited and wanted to know more about the theory of surplus value, ownership of the means of production and so on. I answered all their questions as well as I was able.

We were up all night talking and by morning they were desperate to sell some left-wing newspapers. I provided them with a good stock and, as we left town, they'd already started work building an underground station to sell them outside of.

Back on the Interstate Highway we thumbed a lift from a gang of psychopathic killers on the run from justice; then from a hypocritical preacher; then a young woman who used to teach school but was on

the look-out for some excitement; then a chorus girl who thought she could make it in Hollywood; then a group of Okies whose farm had been repossessed by the bank; then two junkies with fear and loathing in their eyes; then some other people. In this way we reached the wilds of Colorado.

It was good to be in the wilderness.

Before long a big bear came ambling along and we scurried into a cave, frightened for our lives.

'What's the big idea?' said the bear.

Bears do not talk. Everyone knows this. Even in the present-day literary atmosphere of anarchic experimentation with narrative form the introduction of a talking bear will not win you many votes on the Booker Prize selection committee. Let it be said, therefore, before this *oeuvre* gets written off entirely as a contender for literary awards, that this bear, the bear which me and Bobby McGee encountered in Colorado, did not talk. It shouted.

'What's the big idea?' shouted the big, ambling bear in Colorado. 'I'll tell you what the big idea is,' he continued, 'Einstein's Theory of Relativity, that's the big idea. And if you want another big idea, what about Darwin's Theory of Evolution? That's another big idea. And if you want some more big ideas, try some of these for size. Having string in the bathroom for turning the light on so you don't risk electrocution when you've got wet hands. That's a big idea. Auto reverse on cassette players. That's a big idea. Putting different coloured bits of plastic on the top of coat hangers so you can find your size at a glance in the clothing store. That's a big idea. Living in this cave. That's a big idea. More to the point that's my big idea. So get lost.'

'I didn't know bears could talk,' said Bobby.

'He's not talking, he's shouting,' I replied.

'I didn't know bears could shout,' said Bobby.

'Aren't bears supposed to be dangerous?' I said.

'That's propaganda you're believing there,' shouted the bear. 'They said the same about the Indians. Said they were dangerous and scalped people. Propaganda to justify stealing their land. Now they're trying the same stuff on us bears. It ain't none of it true. I ain't going to hurt you. In fact I could even protect and help you. I could

64

warn you of some of the dangers of living out here in the wilderness.'

'What dangers?'

The bear was pensive for a moment. Then he shouted quietly and slowly. 'Well something around here is killing all the elm trees. And it sure as hell ain't me.'

Hollywood, California – Universal Studios Tour Bus.

For myself the most interesting part of the studio tour was the knowledge that the great Albanian writer Klepke Klepke had once worked at Universal Studios – in the Bacon Department. Although he wrote very few short stories, the United States did inspire one of his best, the story known as Bongo Bongo Baby.

BONGO BONGO BABY BY KLEPKE KLEPKE

Translated by Geoffrey Rippon

Saul Kaminsky was a Vietnam Vet. He was twenty-eight but felt like a sixty-year-old, even on a good day. Vietnam had seen to that. Like many Vietnam Vets he had discovered that, by the late sixties, there weren't many people on the Mekong Delta who were interested in having their cats neutered or their budgies' toenails clipped. The work just dried up overnight and so, penniless and disillusioned, Saul returned to New York.

He gave up being a Vet altogether, rented a loft in the Village and lived alone but for a few square yards of fibreglass insulation and a hissing water tank. He decided to devote the rest of his life to zen bongo playing.

He remembered his father who had brought him over from the old country all those years ago.

'We are in America now,' his father used to say, 'And we must learn to be Americans. We must learn to spell "colour" without the "u" and aluminium without an "i".'

'It is so hard to be an American, father,' young Saul had said.

'Most of all,' his father had continued, 'we must learn to talk shit and wear the funny trousers.'

Saul sat in his loft now, looking at his trousers. They were funny all right. They were real funny. Oh yes, he had learned to be an American all right. His nose was filled with the putrid stink that was America. Or maybe something had gotten into the water tank and died.

Eventually Saul found work playing zen bongos in a club off of 52nd Street called the Five Spot, in honour of the owner's skin condition. There were many clubs on 52nd Street at the time: the Three Deuces; Sam's Place; the Workington Trades & Labour Club; and the I-Spy.

Saul played good bongos. He played urgent bongos. In fact it was the very urgency of his bongo playing that first made Natalie think she could score a loan off him. Natalie was a torch singer and desperately needed money to get some PP3s for her torch. She showed the torch to Saul but Saul turned away, his face crumpled in a tortured expression.

'Don't talk to me about torches!' he said.

'Why not?' asked Natalie.

'I just don't want to talk about it.'

Natalie bought him a drink and eventually he unwound.

'When we were in 'Nam . . .' he said, and looked away, unsure whether he could bring himself to continue. He shuddered involuntarily and wiped his mouth with the back of his hand. 'When we were in 'Nam . . . the VC used to . . . sometimes they used to shine torches upwards, under their chins . . . to frighten us.'

'And did it?' asked Natalie.

A big tear emerged from the corner of Sam's eye and trickled down his cheek. Natalie lent him her hanky and he had a good old blow. Then he continued . . .

'Once, one of them . . . the VC . . . one of them put his torch inside his mouth and switched it on. You could still see the light shining through the flesh of his cheek. I don't think a person, even a deadly enemy, should do that sort of thing. I mean, if a small child had seen, he or she might have been tempted to copy and . . . putting torches in your mouth like that . . . it must be dangerous. Apart from the electrical hazards, the glass could shatter and do incalculable damage to the soft palate.'

Natalie nodded, 'I agree, Saul,' she said. 'People shouldn't encourage young children to do dangerous things.'

From then on Saul and Natalie went everywhere together.

THE END

THE FURTHER ADVENTURES OF MICK AND HIS MIDGET POPE.

THE STORY SO FAR: MICK, A TEAK SALESMAN FROM RIPON HAS FOUND A THERMOS-FLASK CONTAINING A MIDGET POPE WHO CAN PERFORM MIRACLES.

TOGETHER THEY SET OUT TO FIND FAME AND FORTUNE...

L'ESCARGOT, A FASHIONABABUBBLE RESTAURANT.

THE 'TIME OUT' FOOD CORRESPONDENT IS OVER THERE.

FUCKIN WHERE?

MORE NEXT WEEK IN THE
THRILLING ADVENTURES OF
MICK AND HIS MIDGET
POPE.

MAY

Brightlights – The Bus of Death.

Spiggly spiggly spoo, diddly diddly doo, doop, doop, dozam da, shlimp, shlamp shan zazazagazz – and dat's jazz!

Recently I attended the funeral of a friend. This old pal of mine had fallen on very hard times and his relatives had had to rely on the government death grant to pay for the funeral – this grant is £35, a measly and miniscule amount which I know terrifies old age pensioners. (Incidentally the term Old Age Pensioners really is a demeaning and patronising term. A better phrase to signify people who have given their best years to their country should be something like 'The Nearly Dead' – that's much more accurate and less patronising.) Anyway, I wouldn't exactly say this funeral I went to was a pauper's funeral but when I got there the grave was being dug by three alsatians.

That's no way to go. We have no choice that we will die, but we can perhaps choose the way. We can hope for a good death. As the eponymous heroine of Graham Greene's *Travels With My Aunt* says – I don't have the book here but it goes something like, 'blah, blah, blah, catholic priest, blah, blah, crying alone in the blah, blahblah. Death is like a wall we can only choose when we meet it blah blah, sin, blah blah.' Or as that other great thinker, Lux Interior, lead singer of The Cramps, remarked when questioned about that band's admiration for the late rock 'n' roller Ricky Nelson: 'What a way to go out man! Freebasin' on ya own airplane!'

A fairly good death should involve a car or motorbike crash, as long as you don't drive or ride one for a living – James Dean, T. E. Lawrence, Camus, Isadora Duncan (strangled by her own scarf wrapped round the back wheel of a Bugatti) all went the right way.

Plane crashes are ignominious unless you're flying the thing or are the rear gunner. But the truly great deaths should contain elements of the bizarre and the comical. For example, Mehmet Shahu, Deputy President of Albania, killed by his boss the eighty-four-year-old President Enver Hoxha during a gunfight over dinner. The vision of those two old men blazing away with heavy service revolvers over the Glishnik Kebab should be enough to make any young person join the Communist Party immediately. Alan Snetterton, the film director, who was stung to death by a manta-ray that he was trying to have sex with, is an example to us all.

The world of buses is shot through with the mythology of death. For example, if you are walking home late one night, maybe tired from a party and you see coming towards you a night bus where no night bus should be, a night bus black as the night, headlights blazing yellow, with a hooded conductor saying 'Room for one more on top', at all costs do not board this bus for this is 'Brightlights' – The Bus of Death. He is seen out of the corner of the eye at all bus disasters, motorway pile-ups, decapitation of double-deckers by low bridges, brake failures and skids. There he is waiting to take his passengers to Hades *via* the River Styx and Cemetery Gates.

Of course the reason that we can contemplate death at all is because we don't at base believe that it will ever happen to us personally: like the piece of toilet graffiti: 'I'm immortal – up to now.' A while ago a magazine asked me what I'd have on my gravestone. After giving it some thought I replied that I would be inclined to have the following inscription: 'Surely there's been some mistake.'

However a Canadian company has just come up with a way for us all to be reminded of our mortality and our insignificance when confronted with the scale of the universe. This company offers, for a fee, to name a star after you or some loved one and have it placed on an astral chart. Then on a clear night you can gaze into the heavens and see the star with your name on it and then, somewhere, in the limitless realms of space and time, the stars like dust, billion on billion, without time, without number, stretching . . . stretching . . . the void . . . dust . . . ni. . . .

The Strange Case of Gullum Gluck or the Old Switcheroo.

One morning David Stafford and I sat stretched out in front of a blazing fire in our central London bachelor apartment, idly discussing what to write for this week's column. Mrs Fishguard, our housekeeper, was clearing away the breakfast things and I was drowsily picking out a Bon Jovi song on my stylophone. 'Why don't we tell them a story from our secret casebook?' said David. 'What, from when we were detectives?' I asked. 'Yeah,' he said. 'What about the case of the "Old Switcheroo"?' 'Okey Dokey,' I said.

So here it is. I'm sure most of you have heard of Camden Council's now disbanded 'Community Detective Service', but just to recap, in 1978 the newly-elected Labour council passed a motion that it shouldn't solely be the privilege of the rich to consult hard-bitten, bourbon-soaked, cynical private detectives. So the 'Community Detective Service' was founded and housed in an annexe of the social-services department, our beat-up 1972 Buick Le Sabre parked incongruously next to the Meals On Wheels vans. We had our own sub-section of NALGO. We were a tough group of men and women – 'Dangerous' David Stafford, first graduate of Sussex University's BA course in Third World Politics, Macramé and Detection; and 'Mad' Lily Tomlin – a tough cookie for sure – one fist of steel, the other of Brie.

The strange case of Gullum Gluck began one dreary Wednesday morning. A beautiful woman came into my office. 'Sorry, I'm half an hour late,' she said. 'Well, I still reckon that's a bit early to start thinking you're pregnant,' I replied. 'Is that what you wanted to see me about?' It wasn't. I should explain at this point that my beat was that part of Camden south of the Euston Road known as 'Little Liverpool', where the Scouse bodegas resound to the clink of Higsons bottles and Echo and The Bunnymen songs. She was from there, Eileen Maginty was her name. She had come south from Liverpool with her husband Tommy six months before that to look for work. No dice. A month previously Tommy had disappeared. A week after that £500 in used notes had come through the door of their bedsit. These weekly payments had continued. She had been getting used to the idea that Tommy had left her, when, wandering past the Royal Opera House the previous night, she had suddenly seen Tommy surrounded by a laughing, glittering group which included Tom Stoppard, Lady Antonia Fraser, Kingsley Amis and A. N. Wilson. (She recognised them from a feature in *Cosmopolitan* entitled 'Fast-moving Reactionary Shitbags of the Eighties'.) They were gone before she could approach but she was insane to find out what an unemployed Liverpool docker was doing in such company. Could I investigate?

I trailed Tom Stoppard for days, from one right-wing soirée to another. Finally at a reading of dissident poetry he introduced us to Albania's leading dissident poet, now in exile – Gullum Gluck. And out stepped Tommy Maginty!

After the reading I spoke to the supposed East European poet. He was laying the naive foreigner on a bit thick. I asked him why he had left Albania. 'Well,' he said, 'An Englishman's home is his castle, but an Albanian's home is his toilet.' I said I was from Liverpool and asked him if he'd ever been there. He replied, 'I haven't but I notice in American football that all the players have their names on the back of their shirts while in British football the players seem to have their names on the front of the shirt, and I notice all the Liverpool team seem to be called 'Crown PaintS'. Without warning I switched from the English I had been speaking to Liverpool 'Scouse' patois as spoken by the cast of 'Brookside'.

'Eh lar,' I said, 'Did you razz dem trainers down da jazzie or wazz da buzzies down de ozzie?'

'Naw ace,' he replied without thinking. 'I kopped da nazzers wit me beef in da lembo . . .'

'Tommy Maginty lah, yooze nicked,' I said. 'What's the story?'

Although I had already guessed most of it, he told me about the old switcheroo. The way the switch works in the entertainment business is like this. If you are in Australia, for instance, you constantly come across entertainers who are billed as 'The Lamp-posts – Britain's top punk band' or 'Dennis Titan-Rocket – England's fastest rising alternative comic'. It's an old trick to go to a foreign country and claim you're an absolutely quadruple enormous star back home. Kelly Monteith, Suzanne Vega and Bruce

Springsteen mean nothing, nada, doodly-squat back home in the States, but in Britain they've managed to become biggies, imported exotica sometimes being more interesting than home-grown talent.

Tommy had worked the switcheroo on himself. Right-wing 'intellectuals' – yer Tom Stoppards and yer Professor Roger Scrutons – don't give a toss for the suffering of the boring, smelly old British working class, but show them a put-upon artiste from the East and they poo their pants with excitement and compassion. The unemployed Tommy had managed to pass himself off as a persecuted poet and had then been showered with money, offers of sex and publishing contracts by reactionary nobs. Mind you, Tommy was really pleased I'd found him. As he said, 'I can't wait to get back to Eileen and me mates for some intelligent conversation. Another few days with these dozy gob-shites and I'd have lost me ollies.'

Get Me An Ambulance.

There's something weird going on out there. Don't lie to me, I know. I heard it on the radio. Usually in the mornings I listen to Radio 1 because I am very, very stupid, but by accident this morning I tuned into Radio 4 and this woman came on and she said she had a warning for somebody called Gail, then she said, 'Silly fishcake, German bite force nine, fuckall travelling west eight miles!' Weird *ou quoi*?

I could have shrugged this off if I hadn't found out a fact, a fact that chilled my blood and made an icy claw grip my heart. This fact is this – Dire Straits are really popular! I know it sounds crazy, I know it's mad, but it's true, goddammit! You see being in show business I read all these trade papers like *Cinema Takings Review*, *Bums on Seats* and *What Novelty* (with a special rubber trumpet pull-out supplement); not to mention the excellent *For What It's Worth* on Channel Four with its regular 'Which?' Best Buy comical red nose feature. So anyway I was flicking through *Bums on Seats* and in a feature on Dire Straits it said that last year Dire Straits did eleven straight nights at Wembley Arena and had sold THIRTY MILLION RECORDS WORLDWIDE!

Well you could have knocked me down with a condom! I mean I'd seen Dire Straits years ago at the Rock Garden and they gave new meaning to the phrase 'Nothing Special'. I'd vaguely followed their music over the years – at a dinner party in Milton Keynes somebody might put 'Brothers In Arms' on the turntable and I'd listen for fifteen minutes and then stamp their turntable into a tiny cube of metal shouting 'Now it really is a compact disc player!' But the more I read the more amazed I became because the charts and the concert halls are all full of adulated bands that are crap and, come to mention it, laughed-at comedians who aren't funny. Why is this? How could this be? I spent a great deal of time thinking about it, too frightened to go out.

Being a Marxist, rather than accept some simple answer, I evolved a complex theory to explain this strange phenomenon. Partly it is a simple question of Marxist supply and demand – somebody has to be number one, no matter what the quality or, to paraphrase H. G. Wells 'In the country of the third-rate, the second-rate does eleven straight nights at Wembley Arena.' But I think it goes deeper than that. I think the mass audience has found that it prefers its heroes actually to be mediocrities rather than people possessed of awesome

"THERE'S SOMETHING FUNNY GOING ON HERE", THOUGHT MR PLIM.

power. After all, the work of genius often needs work to compre-
hend, it requires discrimination and perception of the audience. But
the plodding obviousness of the stadium-playing, compact disc-
selling geriatrics, your Dire Straits and Genesises, requires no
commitment from the listener, just passive acceptance and clapping
their hands when they're told to.

So when Bruce Springsteen, for example, is referred to as a
'genius' it's nonsense. He's just dead popular with a lot of dimmos
because of the unchallenging nature of what he does. A real true
genius would be somebody who was incredibly unpopular, never
sold any records, was fat, rode a bike and had a column in a London
listings magazine.

Thames TV Crew Bus – Euston Road to Hackney City Farm.

Work continues on the children's drama series I am doing for
Thames Television. Set on a community farm in the run-down
inner city it concerns the struggles of the man who runs the farm (i.e.
me) to keep it open despite the efforts of evil council officials. The
series is filmed in a real inner city farm in East London using the real
farm animals and helped by the real farm hands.

I do a lot of acting with the farm animals. One day I was doing a
scene with a cute woolly sheep and I said to the real farm worker 'Say
Mr Real Farm Worker, this is a cute baa-sheep. What's his name?'

'His name's Freddie,' said the farm worker.

A couple of days later we were doing some acting with a farm duck
and one of the child actors said to the real farm worker man, 'Ooh
this is such a sweet darling little duckie. What's its name?'

'It's called Freddie,' said the farm worker.

A couple of days after that we were filming with a goat and I said to
the same man, 'Gosh this really is one of the most charming
delightful goats I've ever seen. What name does it have?'

'Oh that goat,' he replied, 'that goat's name is Freddie.'

'Excuse me Mr Real Farm Worker man, but there seem to be a lot of animals called Freddie running around this farm. I think you just tell soppy people like me that the animals are called Freddie but in fact you don't bother giving the animals names because you aren't soppy about animals and one day you're planning to kill and eat quite a few of them. Isn't that true?'

'That's right, Freddie,' he replied.

National Bus Company: Route 519 – London to Northampton.

An Autobiographical Note

Life is as tedious as a Tyne Tees sitcom and the only way in which a sane and honest person can escape is to hide in a darkened room with the curtains drawn and the doors locked, a bottle of whiskey, a packet of bourbon creams and several back issues of *Wickerwork News* and *Varnish Weekly* at one's side – and devote oneself to the imaginative life.

When I was ten I dreamed of becoming a skating detective. Solving crimes on the frozen canals of Amsterdam in wintertime. I would have a secret radio built into my scarf and, whizzing gracefully along the ice, I would transmit and receive messages from HQ. The other skaters would not suspect my true identity. They would merely think I was a man talking to his scarf.

'Reported break-in at the Van Gogh Museum,' the radio would say, 'Thieves escaping on ski-bikes.'

'Wilco, roger and out!' I would reply and, bending to reduce wind resistance, I would skim along the ice faster than a speeding tram, my eyes ever peeled for the sight of suspicious looking characters on ski-bikes carrying a painting in vibrant yellow hues.

I abandoned this ambition at the age of eleven when I discovered that the Dutch police weren't unionised.

My new ambition was to run away to Malta and join the plain clothes division of the St John's Ambulance Brigade. It sounded like just the sort of tough, pioneering life I craved. I would cut a dashing

78

figure walking round the Maltese streets with nothing but a discreet lapel badge to disclose my vocation. In fact, the collar badge would contain a secret radio transmitter with which I would transmit and receive messages from HQ.

'Accident with a bread knife in Rupert Square,' the radio would say.

'Wilco, roger and out,' I would reply and suddenly, to the surprise of innocent passers-by, my lapel badge/secret radio would expand and turn itself into a gyrocopter which would whisk me skywards and on to Rupert Square in the twinkling of an eye.

Fortunately I have been able to achieve this ambition. So if you happen to attend one of my performances and I either don't turn up or seem to be mumbling to myself and leave the stage very suddenly after a couple of minutes and don't return, you will know that my secret radio has called me out on an errand of mercy in Malta. I hope that, should this situation arise, you will not be churlish about it and make a fuss and ask for your money back.

Meanwhile back on the Northampton bus I shouted 'Pshaag!', tore the book I was reading in two and flung it across the bus. I get so annoyed with authors. I had been reading Howard Jacobson's *Coming From Behind* – 'Why,' I raged, 'Can't writers have the guts to set their writing in real exciting cities, rather than creating bloody whimsical fictional towns with stupid names like "Wolverthorpe" and "Fulchester"?'

Just at that moment the bus pulled into the outskirts of Bonkersley. We crossed the new bridge which spans the River Bonk, skirted the sandstone bluffs of Mount Bink, cruised past Bonkersley Swamp and into the centre of town, finally stopping at Bonkersley Bus Station.

I was visiting the small market town of Bonkersley in the county of South Bonkshire to stay with my Uncle Ron. Recently Uncle Ron had broken his neck in twenty-seven places and since then he'd never looked back. An unlucky, shabby little man, he was heavily tattooed – he had 'loser' written all over him. Growing up in a socialist family in the heady optimistic days of the 1930s Uncle Ron had fallen in with the then popular theory that if mankind spoke one common language compiled from the leading languages of the world, shared understanding would result in an end to war, suffering and exploitation. Esperanto was the common pre-war lingua franca, but there was also Polylingua which was what Uncle Ron had learned. The Polylingualists and the Esperantists used to meet in Bonkersley Market Square on a Saturday night and would fight each other with chains, knives and the starting handles from trams.

Nevertheless Uncle Ron refused to speak anything except Polylingua. Luckily I am proficient in this. In fact I can speak sixteen languages: I don't know what the fuck I'm saying, but I can speak 'em.

'*Bueno Mungo!*' said Uncle Ron.

'*Bueno Mungo, Unclo Ronno!*' I said, '*How est-vous y Janet et John? Como bongo delenda ist jam forte bongo?*'

'*Tea kettle bladder. Arsehole chipstick meo bongo. Merde bauhaus banana,*' replied Uncle Ron.

(Don't worry about understanding this. Apart from being a Polylingualist, Uncle Ron is also completely mad.)

Uncle Ron lives on a smallholding in the countryside just outside Bonkersley. He retired there to start a fish farm but he was having difficulty getting them planted. But mainly he had an interesting

WE INTERRUPT THIS COLUMN WITH AN URGENT SAFETY NOTICE. ANYONE WHO BOUGHT A FUTON FROM THE NAGASAKI FUTON COMPANY SHOULD RETURN THIS TO THE SHOP IMMEDIATELY AS A SERIOUS DESIGN FAULT COULD RESULT IN THE OWNER LOOKING LIKE A STUPID PRAT. THANK YOU. WE NOW RETURN YOU TO ALEXEI SAYLE'S GREAT BUS JOURNEYS OF THE WORLD.

... with an octopus, which was really the funniest thing I've ever seen.

JUNE

Airport Link Bus – Auckland Airport to Regent Hotel, Swanson Street, Auckland.

Early June saw me boarding an Air New Zealand Jumbo, bound for the land of the long white cloud.

Apart from being an inveterate traveller on buses, the fact is I am also a bit of a bus spotter. I have come to New Zealand to do some work and study some of the interesting old buses they have here.

New Zealand is in many ways like being in Britain ten or twenty years ago. For instance, because cars are expensive to import, people hang onto them for a long time so the roads are full of extinct brands of British cars: old Triumphs, Hillmans, Humbers and Rileys trundle at stately speeds along the modern motorways.

Also the Kiwi TV channels buy most of their programmes from Britain but to get them cheap they wait until they are a few years old, so the TV screens here are crammed with antique episodes of *The Brothers*, *Muffin the Mule* and *Steptoe and Son*.

And the NZ television stations also buy most of their news output from Britain, but again, to save money, they buy up old bulletins from the BBC and ITN so last night's headlines at nine o'clock were Harold Wilson resigning, Wolves topping the English First Division and UK beer prices going up to two shillings a pint.

Route No. 7 – Swanson Street to Kiwi Komedy Kabaret, Anzac Avenue, Auckland.

Being something of a father figure to a new generation of young comedians all over the world, on my visits to various comedy clubs

81

here in Kiwi land, I have been surrounded by crowds of aspiring funny persons all begging my advice on various aspects of stand-up comedy.

I am always happy to look at the work of young comedians and if they show any signs of talent at all I tell them they are totally useless and should give up immediately. (I don't want the competition.)

The other advice I give is that a comedian should always look smart and wear a suit – but not a bunny suit with floppy ears.

One rule of comedy that I am very serious about though is the Rule of Three. The Rule of Three means that if you are either doing stand-up comedy or writing comedy and you want to make a list of funny things, then for some reason a list of three things is much funnier than a list of two things or a list of four things or five things. Unfortunately there are people employed on newspapers called 'subs' or sub-editors. It is the job of these people to edit, shape and prune people's writing so that it doesn't make any sense. When I write I often make a list of three hilarious funny things. The subs on the *Sunday Mirror* then chop out one of the funny things, leaving a sad list of only two mildly funny things. Madness! They really must stop doing this! There are three reasons why they must stop: it spoils the humour of my writing, it's a gross interference with the work of a major artist and most important of all it's

NZ Tours: Auckland to Te Puke, Home of 'Kiwifruit Country' (The Kiwifruit Capital of the World).

While New Zealand may be in a metaphorical time warp, I have personal evidence that real time warps do exist. I saw this film once where a man somehow fell through a time warp and landed in the 'next' day. While he was there he got his hands on a newspaper so that when he was flipped back to his own time he was then in possession of 'tomorrow's' paper. He then did the obvious thing which was to make loads of bets at the bookies because of course he already had all the results of tomorrow's races and he made a fortune.

A similar thing happened to me. While on a brass rubbing holiday in Shrewsbury, I also fell through a crack in the space-time continuum which was just outside the British Home Stores and I landed in 'next' week. Unfortunately before the laws of physics grabbed me back, all I could get my hands on was a copy of next month's *The World of Interiors*.

When I got back to 'today' – my own time – I rushed down to the book-makers and tried to place a ten pound bet on what was going to be screamingly fashionable in silk curtains and wallcoverings during the spring season. But the bookie wasn't interested.

The other day I saw a British television show called the *Paul Daniels Magic Show*. In this show a short man with a funny haircut – Paul Daniels – performs what you might call 'magic' tricks.

For instance, he got a man called Ken, who he's never met before, to set his watch to a certain time and then Paul put his own watch (which told a different time to Ken's) with Ken's in a bag and when the watches came out, both told the same time!

Also he made the hankies of two Asian women disappear and then reappear in interesting and strange places. He also did something astonishing with a wooden duck and some playing cards.

Now, try as hard as I might to see how the incredible effects were achieved, I couldn't. I was boggled. I can only conclude that there was no trick, no sleight of hand involved: that this very small man with the odd haircut really does have magical powers, that he does these things through the use of superhuman, unearthly psychic abilities not granted to us mere mortals.

But the point is, seeing as Paul Daniels does have magical powers, why, oh why, is he frittering them away on some tacky television show? Come on Paul! For God's sake! The world is racked with plague, famine and pestilence; unrest and corruption are rife, the media is full of trivia and lies and yet, and yet, you squander your incredible powers on tricks with wooden ducks and messing about with Asians' hankies!

I beg you Paul, use your magical powers to help the world now!

Here it is! The greatest short story competition of all time. All other short story competitions are fucking crap compared to the 'Great Bus Journeys of the World' Short Story Competition, because the Great Bus Journeys Competition isn't looking for the best written short story or the most elegant or interesting or dialectic short story. No! This is a proper competition – we're looking for the shortest short story. The story of last year's winner (Jeffrey Archer of The 'Where's My Tortoise' Private Mental Home, Dorset) on the theme of urban alienation was a thrilling eight words long and included the exciting words 'dog', 'bog' and 'Commonwealth Eminent Persons Group'. First prize in the competition this year is an all-expenses-paid night on the town with Auberon Waugh – so let's see those seven-word opuses rolling in!

Of late, writing is taking up more and more of my time. I do mainly poems and short stories and recently I've been delighted to have several of my poems published – in this year's Argos catalogue.

Six Plugs – £4.95

is perhaps one of my best efforts. Also:

Garden Hose, 15 metres – £29.75 (Batteries Not Included)

was said in the *London Review of Books* to be 'poignantly, achingly, sad. When finally the end is reached and we see the "Hoselok R tap attachment", I, for one was filled with a tremendous and appalling sense of loss.' – *Melvyn Bragg*. But perhaps my finest work is reproduced opposite from the Grattans Catalogue of 1985.

I got into a bit of trouble in the publishing world a few years ago. You see, I mistakenly thought the book biz was like the record biz and the distribution of a few cheap digital watches could get my book to the top of the charts. But, of course, many booksellers are so inefficient that even if they took bribes they couldn't rig the charts.

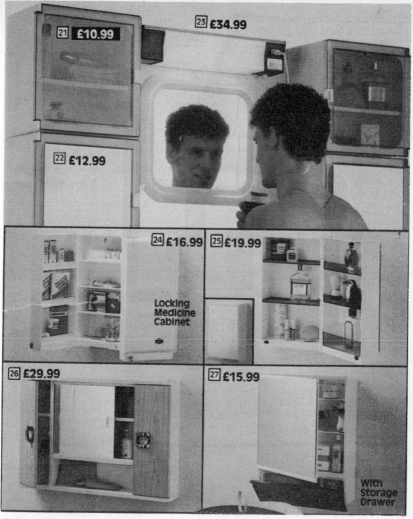

23 Terrific modular bathroom cabinet including plastic mirror into which Giles stared, the nightmarish visions of Miranda's words echoing again and again in his head. He held the razor to his throat. "Eternity?" he thought. "Blackness?" Size: 610 x 260 x 260mm approx. (Batteries not included.)

WW 22 87 Cabinet	£34.99
	35 wks £1.00

25 Attractive single mirror door bathroom cabinet from the Gilac range in white with a gold look decorative strip. Both door and cabinet have adjustable shelves to

26 Bathroom cabinet with two side cupboards, pine finish doors and sliding mirrors over an open shelf. A large capacity cabinet at a reasonable price. Comes packed flat for easy home assembly. Size: 18½ x 27¾ x 5ins

*WW 23 07 Cabinet	£29.99
	20 wks £1.50

27 A superbly styled single door cabinet with generous and varied shelving with smoke fall front drawer and child safety device. Manufactured in polystyrene. Size: 35½ x 46 x 14cms approx.

*WW 23 86 Cabinet	£15.99

Finally I burst into the room where the Booker Prize Jury was sitting, carrying half a pound of coke and twenty colour televisions, shouting 'Whatever J. G. Ballard's offering, I'll double it!' So I've had to get out of the snooty end of fiction and instead I've decided to write a best-selling block-buster that you buy at supermarkets and bus stations. It'll be called something like *Hijack the Pope* or *A Brick Before Midnight*. Authoritative people say that in writing film scripts, books, plays, whatever – the ending, the last ten minutes or the last few pages are the most important of all. If a film, for instance, has a cracking last ten minutes the audience will often forgive the tedium of the rest. With this in mind I have decided to write the end of my block-busting, best-selling novel first and then figure out what it's all about later. So here, right now, we present the last ball-boggling, thrilling page of *Shades of Black Eternity* by Jeffrey Sayle (my secret pen-name):

helicopter blades on Treadgold's treasured Burberry.

Finally, a shower of sparks ignited the gorse on the headland. There was the slight thud of a contained explosion. Then everything was quiet except for the rustling of the burning gorse and the mad humming of Tsisi.

That night there were two sunsets. The sky burned red in the east as well as the west and with it burned the remains of Hendricks, a couple of acres of broadleaved woodland, the blueprints of an elasticated garage and, most important of all, a hope. A hope that something good, something lasting, something purposeful, could come out of this unholy mess we had learnt to call 'Operation Labelling Regulations'.

By morning all that remained was the asbestos label from Hilary's gas cape.

In the observation trench Tsisi lit two cigarettes and with them she lit a torch in my heart that could not be extinguished. At last I understood what the boys at school had meant when they talked of love. Now I only had to find out what they had meant when they spoke of the Blue Goldfish.

JULY

London Regional Transport: Route 73 – Stoke Newington to Hammersmith Broadway.

As soon as I got back to Britain from New Zealand I had to jump on a number 73 and head straight for my accountants. My financial affairs were in a mess. I'd lost a lot of my money through bad investments. I'd put all my money into a string of shops, 'Big Alexei's High Street Poison Gas, Nuclear Weapons and Cocaine Shop' – well, nobody told me it was against the fucking law! The rest of my money I put into a self-service massage parlour. Then I formed a company. When you form a company you have to put other people that you can trust on the board. So I put my Gran, my Uncle Ted and my rubber plant in as co-directors. However, after a while I found that my Gran was trying to trade in me on the Unlisted Securities Market; Uncle Ted was conspiring with Rupert Murdoch to take me over; and the rubber plant was heavily involved in insider dealing. Quickly I turned the rubber plant in to the Inland Revenue; I had Gran arrested; and I took out a contract on Uncle Ted. Unfortunately the contract I took out was a catering contract, so now, twice a week, he gets a spread of sandwiches, mixed salad and a selection of French fancies.

There is a myth that accountants are dull – not true. Accountants are well groovy. Those dudes that hang round downtown US streets in snap-brimmed pink hats and fur-lined Lincoln Continentals are accountants. Most of the Ray-Banned, shark-skin suited audience for Courtney Pine's Jazz Warriors are accountants. See that woman on the 1200cc Moto Guzzi coming up in the rear-view mirror – she's an accountant.

Mine was a rock-biz accountant. He was a whiz at clever tax evasion schemes, my accountant. One time he persuaded a leading pop star to speak nothing but Serbo-Croat, dress in Ruritanian fancy uniforms and kick poor people for a year. My accountant then convinced the Customs and Excise that the pop star was in fact the last King of Yugoslavia – he was then able to re-claim all the VAT paid on diesel fuel by the fourth German Panzer Division in 1943 and was also able to write off the cost of the invasion of Crete as a tax loss. For nine months my accountant had me running round the streets dressed only in my underpants waving a balloon on a stick – but then I found out that was just because he didn't like me.

Talking of Balkan kings, I was telling somebody the other day, and honest to God this is true, that in the '20s the royal line in Albania died out so they held a referendum to find out who the people wanted to rule them. The upshot of this was that the people of Albania requested C. B. Fry, Arsenal Centre Forward and England cricketer, to be their new king. Being busy with the test series, C.B. declined and in time the infamous King Zog (Also true! Just look it up if you don't fucking believe me – big nose!) was appointed King of Albania with disastrous results. However, between C. B. Fry and King Zog, Albania had another ruler who has left his mark even on the modern Balkan state. The people's second choice for King and also Leader of the Legislative Assembly was a British musician and leading member of the Musicians' Union, a Mr Reg 'Sticks' McMurdo – drummer with the Lew Abrahams Jazz Bandits. Having just finished a season playing the Starlight Room at the Bolton Locarno he was free and accepted the job with alacrity. Although the Legislative Assembly has seen many changes since 1923, Reg McMurdo's influence is still very much in evidence.

While the Legislative Assembly is in session (a basic session being three hours) members of the Assembly are entitled to a minimum of £53 for straight sound recording or £58.50 if the session is for Independent Television. During this time members are allowed to make one speech. If they speak twice they are entitled to a doubling fee of £7.95. If they are required to speak both for and against the motion then they may be engaged for a two hour over-dubbing session for a fee of £46.20. A maximum of two motions may be debated during this time. Overtime (for completion of any work commenced during the session and with the agreement of the members) is paid at the rate of £6.90 per 15-minute unit. Sub-committees are paid at Casual Gig rates.

The Albanian parliament is the only one in the world to wear matching red blazers and sit behind glittering music desks with a monogrammed 'LA' (for Legislative Assembly). They are also the only nation in the world to have the words 'Home Taping is Killing Music' enshrined as Article One of the constitution.

AUGUST

PERU – NORWAY – ZAIRE – USSR

Yes! Here we are again – as large as life and as ninth as cheerful. All of July has been spent by myself and, in much smaller letters, David Stafford, scouring the world of buses, scanning the globe to bring you:

STRANGER THAN FICTION!

AMAZING BUT TRUE BUS STORIES FROM ALL PARTS OF THE WORLD!!

PERU

The Bleeding Bus of Lima.

For 364 days of the year the 27b (City Square to the Pen and Inca) is a perfectly normal Peruvian bus transporting the citizens of Lima about their day-to-day affairs. Once a year, however, on the anniversary of the martyrdom of Santa Cathy, the bus bleeds.

Santa Cathy was born Cathy Eusebio, a Peruvian girl who worked in an alarm clock factory. When she was fourteen she saw visions and heard bells and the local priest, impressed by her religious fervour, used his influence to get her a place as a novice in the very exclusive Convent of the Little Sisters of Psychiatrically Dubious Self Denigration.

Cathy worked hard at the Convent and within five years she had been appointed chief bullwhip instructress. Then, one day, while practising her humble craft in the Indiana Jones Detention Wing of the Convent, she had another vision. She saw a strange ship which floated in the sky and inside the ship were men and women. One of the men started coughing and suddenly his chest exploded and a monster came out of it. And in the end Ian Holm turned out to be an android and wires came out of his head and Sigourney Weaver was left on her own and she put a space suit on and opened the airlock so that the monster was sucked out into space.

As a result of this vision Cathy became a travelling sister. She pawned all her possessions and gave the pawn tickets to the poor. She preached in the public squares and told the people to forget their wicked ways, to turn to the path of righteousness and to improve their mid-field playing.

Then, one day, while she was preaching in the City Square in Lima, a 27b came round the corner doing no more than about twenty miles per hour. The driver jammed on his anchors but it was too late. The relic collectors moved in and before long every church in Peru had a bit of Cathy. And thus it is that every year on the anniversary of her martyrdom, the 27b bleeds.

Some people think it might be brake fluid.

NORWAY

The Hammerfest Tree Sprites.

The people of Hammerfest in Northern Norway believe that bus conductors are Tree Sprites. The conductors encourage them in this belief. It means that, in general, passengers are more likely to embark and disembark in an orderly fashion and less likely to spit for fear of the terrible mischief that the Tree Sprites will visit upon them. The conductors are also from time to time given small votive offerings of seed cake and aquavit which, as they put it, don't come at all amiss on a cold Hammerfest morning.

ZAIRE

The Singing Bus of Mbuji-Mayi.

In Mbuji-Mayi there is a bus that sings old Heaven 17 numbers. Its version of 'We Don't Need This Fascist Groove Thang' recently got to number seven in the Central African hit parade. Mechanics and Transport Scientists have examined the bus and, so far, have come up with no satisfactory explanation of this phenomenon. The bus lists amongst its likes big tyres and sensitive drivers and its ambition is to come off the road and concentrate on a recording career.

USSR

When myself and, in much smaller letters, David Stafford arrived in Moscow we were entranced to learn from the great folklorist B. V. Radchenko of the *Two Thousand Tales of U. M. Zaporets.* U. M. Zaporets was a clerk in the Ministry of Jam who, in June 1938, was called before the conscription board. In order to avoid being called up into the army, U. M. Zaporets decided to convince the conscription board that he was completely mad. To achieve this end he told them a bizarre story, 'The Man Who Mistook His Wife For An Ironing Board'. The conscription board was so taken with this story that they called him back every day for many years to hear a different story, thus forming a body of work similar to *The Arabian Nights.* Several of the stories concern buses and here we reprint one:

The Odd Dream of I. N. Skytyvkar

In 1937 I. N. Skytyvkar, a packaging operative at the Velikij Ust'Ug Fishpaste Collective dreamed that he was sitting on a number 19 bus on a trip to visit his married sister in Kotlas.

When he woke up he was indeed on a number 19 bus going to Kotlas, but he was not going to visit his married sister – because to his knowledge at the time he had never had a married sister. When he told his mother about this strange dream she broke down and confessed that, before he was born, before she had married his father, she had had a bastard child, a daughter, who she believed had been carried off and eaten by various members of the pre-revolutionary land-owning classes.

I. N. Skytyvkar wondered whether his mother was right. Perhaps the daughter, his half-sister, had not been eaten by the Kulaks after all? Perhaps she was, after all, alive and married and living in Kotlas as his dream foretold?

So I. N. Skytyvkar sent a letter to the Old Codgers column in *Pravda* telling his story and asking, if the sister should read the letter, that she contact him.

By a miracle the daughter did read the letter and sent I. N. Skytyvkar a postcard, care of the Fishpaste Collective, saying that she was alive and well but, strangely, unmarried.

When I. N. Skytyvkar told his mother of the postcard, his mother broke down again and confessed that she had also had another bastard daughter who she believed had been carried off by wolves in the hard winter of 1902.

Perhaps, thought I. N. Skytyvkar, he had two half-sisters, both living in Kotlas? One an unmarried *Pravda* reader, previously thought to have been eaten by Kulaks, and the other married but possibly somewhat lupine in behaviour owing to the fact that she had been suckled by a she-wolf?

I. N. Skytyvkar decided to travel to Kotlas and investigate for himself. Accordingly the following day he caught the number 19 Velikij Ust'Ug to Kotlas bus. While sitting on the bus he fell asleep and had a dream. He dreamed that both his half-sisters, the unmarried and the wolfish one, met him in a laundry and told him that their mother had killed his father by locking him in an unheated dacha while the lake was hard with frost.

I. N. Skytyvkar woke up and abandoned his quest to find his half-sisters. Instead he swore an oath of vengeance against his mother. From the shores of the Baltic to the Ural Mountains he would hunt her and exact his blood revenge for the treacherous murder of his father.

When he got home his mother was burnishing the samovar. I. N. Skytyvkar confronted her with his dream. His mother was afraid. She broke down and confessed that she had indeed murdered his father in the way the dream-sisters had described. She swore, however, that the murder was a mercy killing. While out collecting wild beetroot in the Koplova forest, his father had been savagely gored by elks and a fragment of elk horn had lodged in his brain bringing a great madness upon him. In his madness he believed he was Jelly Roll Morton, the New Orleans pianist and bandleader. He would run through the streets shouting, 'I invented Jazz. It was me. I invented it while playing piano in a Basin Street brothel. And the white people stole it from me.' His behaviour was attracting attention from the Tsarist Secret Police, the notorious Chaka Kan, and she knew that if the Chaka Kan caught up with him they would send him to the penal colony of Ostrov Kolguev in the wild, cold Barents Sea. Rather than see him come to this end, she decided to kill him by locking him in the unheated dacha of which his dream-sisters had told.

As the mother was telling this tale, the door sprang open and a wolf bounded in. And yet it was not a wolf. It was the married half-sister from Kotlas. The wolf-woman said that the mother was lying, that she was a black-hearted devil who had sold one of her daughters to the Kulaks, thrown the second to the wolves, killed her husband and brought up her only son badly, so that he often became a little confused on buses.

I. N. Skytyvkar now became very confused. Was his mother lying or was his half-sister, dream-sister, wolf-sister telling untruths because she wanted him to kill the mother so that she could feast her pack on the carcase?

It was then that I. N. Skytyvkar recalled a rhyme from his childhood:

He, me, you,
Men are untrue.
Fee, fee, fi,
The wolf cannot lie.

95

And, whispering this rhyme over and over again, he seized an axe and struck his mother dead.

As the first blow was struck, the half-sister, dream-sister, wolf-woman, changed and turned into a Political Commissar from the Kirov Soviet.

The Commissar smiled and put a hand on I. N. Skytyvkar's arm. 'Embrace me, worthy comrade,' said the Commissar. 'Your experiences over the past months culminating in this brutal slaying of your mother have been in the nature of a test – a test of your will, your moral strength and, above all, your understanding of Marxist –Leninist teaching. You may think that the test involving you, as it has done, in strange dreams and matricide has been a little unfair. But take it from me that it is only through tests such as these that we can find people worthy of high office in serving the people of the Soviet Socialist Republic . . . Embrace me yet again, I. N. Skytyvkar, no longer Packing Operative but Packing Supervisor Grade Three.'

Crazy Ken's Coaches: Motorway Express Service – London to Hull.

A few pages back I mentioned that because of the inordinate amount of attention TV producers, editors of London listings magazines, the IBA etc. pay to letters 'written in' by loonies, I had started writing pseudonymous letters about my column to the *Time Out* letters page. All the letters ever written about my column were written by me. However, you may have noticed that there haven't been any letters for a while. Let me explain – at first I wrote letters praising myself, then for variety I started slagging myself off. That's when the trouble started. The letters I wrote became more and more abusive to myself. I stopped writing to *Time Out* but, since I knew my home address, I started writing there; long loony scribbles in coloured felt-tip pen would arrive by every post.

Dear Alexei,
You are just a cheap fat rip-off of the great Ben Elton,
Signed, One Who Knows.

Dear Alexei,
You are the lowest form of pond scum ever to emerge from a
drain,
Love, Mum

Dear Cacky,
Listen, I know you. You drove past me and Mr Trumbaur in a
Land-Rover the other day and looked at us funny. Listen Me
and Mr Trumbaur got a feely-thing that can use psychic brain
power to re-arrange molecules. Mr Trumbaur's also got a
folding-up walking stick and a lucky key-ring and we've got a
special hiding place in the cupboard under your sink. The next
time you come looking for the spare Liquid Gumption we'll be
ready for you. Watch it.
A Pal.

Then I started playing nasty tricks on myself.

Dear Porky-Git,
Guess who put your oven gloves down the lavvy? Ha! Ha! Ha!
A Friend.

Next I stuffed rags soaked in Mr Sheen through my letter box and
tried to light them. Finally I started waiting for myself when I got
home and beating myself up. I decided I had to get away so I caught
the first stage out of town – in this case a cut-price coach to Hull.
    This privatisation and de-regulation is a wonderful thing. Once
upon a time the only inter-city bus services were run by the
monolithic National Bus Company, but in these free-enterprise
days an entrepreneur like Krazy Ken can kit out his Austin A35 van

and hit the highway plying for hire high and low. And the passengers need have no fear for their safety: standards of maintenance and driver hours are strictly supervised by the Bus Users' Supervisory Committee. This powerful organisation is headed by Lord Justice Mandingo-Hubblesprout. Also on the committee are a man called Len and a white rabbit called Mickey. The supervisory committee has tremendous powers to punish offenders – they can either be made to stand in the corner or go to bed early without their supper if they've been very naughty and actually killed lots of people. The committee can be contacted c/o Mickey's Hutch, Back of Mrs Wipple's House, Rayleigh Grove, Essex.

Privatisation has its humane side too. In recent years many gloomy and depressing mental homes have been closed down and in a radical move the mentally ill are now being more closely integrated into the community by being allowed to wander the streets all day, shouting at windows and rootling in dustbins for food. The best scam going these days is the farming of old people. Enormous grants are available for anybody who wants to open a private nursing or old people's home. I am on my way to one scheme I myself am involved in, situated at Dothepensioners Hall, a lovely ex-mental home in North Yorkshire. Lest I be accused of heartless profiteering, I have gone to great lengths to hire many distinguished consultants – notably a Mr Bernard Matthews of Norfolk.

De-regulation in one industry can also benefit another industry. The opening up of the gas industry which now allows any lunatic with a screwdriver and some old garden hose to fit your gas fire should greatly benefit the fire service when it too is privatised.

Entrepreneurs like myself feel it is absolutely vital that the taxpayer is not burdened with the cost of inefficient, parasitic and out-moded enterprises – that is why I am lobbying the Department of Trade and Industry to immediately privatise the Royal Family. Then anybody who wanted to be patronised by an in-bred stick insect could buy shares and pay for it themselves.

Suddenly on the coach there was a tremendous bang as one of the old tractor tyres Ken had been using blew out. Through skilful use of letting go of the steering wheel we all managed to end up dead.

A USEFUL PROVERB

Here's a useful proverb:

'You don't keep a dog and shit on the carpet yourself.'

Monsieur Aubergine

L'HOMME QUI EST COMME UNE
LEGUME. (EN SIX FAÇON DIFFERENTES.)

* MONSIEUR AUBERGINE - THE MAN WHO IS LIKE
A VEGETABLE. (IN SIX DIFFERENT WAYS)

MONSIEUR AUBEGINE CE DECIDE DE JOIGNER LA
LEGION ETRANGÈRE.

* M. AUBERGINE DECIDES TO JOIN
THE FOREIGN LEGION.

MAIS IL PREND LE SERJEANT POUR UN HERRISON.

* BUT HE MISTAKES THE SERGEANT FOR A HEDGEHOG.

ET D'AILLEURS IL EST TEMPS POUR SA LEÇON DE PLONGE A SUBA.

* AND ANYWAY IT IS TIME FOR HIS SCUBA-DIVING LESSONS.

People have again been clamouring for my fashion advice. So my tip this week is – Spats are back! But whatever you do, don't get mixed up between spats and sprats. Spats are a kind of celluloid cover worn over shoes which were originally very popular in the twenties; sprats are small fish. Under no circumstances wear small fish on your shoes. Wearing small fish on your shoes has been right out of fashion since 1981.

I'm asking my fellow members of the tabloid press to stop spreading these rumours about me and Janet Jackson (chart-topping sister of Michael). Sure, Janet and I see each other from time to time, but we are both busy international stars – she has her platinum albums and sell-out concerts and I have my page in the *Sunday Mirror* – and we are just looking for a few friendly laughs together, fitted into our busy international schedules. Honestly, there is no emotional involvement, so just stop saying these things, fellas. OK?

SEPTEMBER

On Ideology.

The strength of Marxism as a didactic, pragmatic ideology is that it is a synthesis – a dazzling mixture of philosophy and economics which now found the basis of the governmental systems of half the world.

The problem, the flaw, is not Marxism's ability to induce revolution but rather its inability to prevent the subsequent betrayal of that revolution.

In the pre-revolutionary state it is in the interests of the revolutionary Marxists to try and instill in the masses scepticism, clarity of thought, a questioning attitude to the workings of the state and a determination to change things for the better. In the post-revolutionary state these fine attributes suddenly become unwanted by the inevitable ruling clique. For the masses dogma and hero-worship replace scepticism and, for the individual, freedom of thought is replaced by state terror.

Thus it is that the deficiency of Marxism is not concerned with the broad sweep of human affairs – the clash of class forces or the world-wide extraction of profit – but rather its weakness lies with its failure to cope with the minutiae of human dynamics. Revolutions are betrayed by small numbers of power-hungry deviants – Stalin, Kim Il Sung in North Korea, Enver Hoxha in Albania etc etc – who seize the revolution and pervert it to their own ends. For Marxism to produce a governmental system which is superior to capitalism and not merely a mirror of it, we need to add to the synthesis so that the ideology can both deter the seizure of power by small groups and prevent the acceptance of inflexible thought, cult of the personality, consumerism etc.

What then, firstly, is lacking in Marxism that leaves it vulnerable to erosion by dictators? I suggest for the answer to this we should turn to the greatest of French philosophers, Albert Camus. It is now a well-known fact that in his early days Camus had a promising career as goalkeeper for the Club Racing Universitaire Algerois (RUA). It was only TB that prevented him being selected for the national side. It is not so well known that his mentor, Jean Grenier, was also a very useful winger and encouraged Camus's love of football. It is also little known how many other great thinkers have been deeply involved in sport – Robert Mugabe, for example, came second in the under 2-litre class in the 1967 East Africa Safari Rally driving a works-sponsored Hillman Imp. It was only a sprung cam-shaft housing (a common fault on early Imps) that prevented him winning outright. (And who knows what effect that would have had on the post-imperialist history of Africa?) Nadezhda Krupskaya was a useful hurdler. On his arrival in the United States Albert Einstein played several seasons as pitcher for the Daytona Ramrods and it was only with great reluctance that he devoted himself full-time to nuclear fission. There are many other examples.

For example, I myself am Bobby Robson's secret love child and followed my dad into professional football, as you all know. Conversely, many sportsmen are great writers and thinkers: Gary Bailey (Former Man Utd goalkeeper) is a PhD in Computer Sciences and Vinny 'Madman' Jones (Wimbledon F.C.) has written several learned monographs on Etruscan pottery.

But to return to Camus, he once said 'Everything I know, I learned from football', and the point I am trying to make is that with deep immersion in sport (especially soccer and cycling) a great understanding of the world follows. Therefore if we add 'sportism' to the synthesis of philosophy and economics the rise of tyrants is subverted.

Secondly, we need to counter the spread in the post-revolutionary state of blind dogma and devotion, lack of scepticism and state-sponsored terror. The answer to this problem is 'humourism'. I have written before how a genuine sense of humour, especially including irony and sarcasm, is an antidote to all things pretentious. For example, if when Lenin uttered the chilling words 'Liberty is precious – so precious that it must be rationed', everybody present had burst into hysterical laughter, made farty noises and wiggled their ears, then the history of the Soviet Union would have been very different.

So I propose that the post-revolutionary workers' state will be run on the principles of the Communist Party of Britain (Marxist-Sportist-Humourist). Party meetings will consist half of discussions of football tactics, golf technique and so on and half of group and individual humour sessions – lessons in 'taking the piss', irony, farce, sarcasm, *droleur*, wittiness, mateyness, chumminess and giggling, guffawing and snorting. Anybody who isn't interested in sport or who doesn't have a sense of humour will, of course, be executed.

NAMES – A SPECIAL ANNOUNCEMENT

It has come to my notice that sometimes names are not shared out equally. For instance while Paul Simon has got two first names, Harrison Ford has got two second names.

While Jean-Paul Sartre, Hugh Trevor Roper and Lesley Anne Down have all got two first names and one second name, Nancy Banks-Smith, Sammy Davis Junior and Andrew Lloyd Webber have all got one first name and two second names.

Norman St John Stevas has got two first names and a second name and a St, Sting and Sade have only got one name each and Meryl Streep hasn't got anything that anybody in their right mind would call a name at all.

The law should immediately be changed so that everybody has two names each – one first name and one second name. Thus those with two first names will pool their names and those with two second names will share the results. Paul Simon will become Paul Harrison and Harrison Ford will become Simon Ford.

Jean-Paul Sartre will be known (on memorials etc.) as Paul Sartre, Lesley Anne Down as Anne Down, Hugh Trevor Roper as Trevor Roper, Nancy Banks-Smith as Nancy Smith, Sammy Davis Junior as Sammy Junior, Andrew Lloyd Webber as Andrew Webber and

Norman St John Stevas as Norman Stevas. This will create a surplus of names from which names falling short of total requirements can be completed.

Thus Sting will take over the Jean left over from Paul Sartre and become Jean Sting; Sade can have the Banks left from Nancy Smith to become Sade Banks; and Meryl Streep can become Trevor Davis. Also there will be a surplus of names sufficient to complete one complete new person, Lesley Lloyd, and a St John.

Thank you for your attention.

Nottingham Transport C3: City Centre Hoppnstopnshoppa.

Brewers have three styles when they 'do up' (or rather 'mess up') a pub. One is 'Old Fashioned'. This involves covering the outside of the pub in medieval/Victorian style gibberish. 'Hottye Pyes' will be written in big squiggly gold letters. Or 'Fyne Wines and Porters For the Replenishment and Delectation of Travellers'.

In Nottingham I fancied a hot pie so I went into a pub which said 'Hottye Pyes, Cooked and Cured Hammes', and asked for the same. They looked at me as if I was barmy and was asking for a grilled antelope.

All they had, like every other pub, was rolls or stale moussaka. When the brewers write 'Olde Worlde' nonsense outside their pubs they could at least be honest. They should write 'Ye Noisiest Videyo Machines in All of Ye Christendom' or 'Fynest Watery Lagers For All Ye Yobbes in Ye Anoraks' and 'Munificent Microwaved Moussaka and Olde Englyshe Chilli Con Carneys Serveyed by Ye Formica Foodye Barre.'

OCTOBER

Hotel Paraiso, Calle del Cojo, Barrio del Retiro,
Caracas, Venezuela.

The rain falls softly in a fine mist on the street outside, making no sound. But there is nevertheless sound aplenty; the cries of the whores and the fruit-sellers in the street outside this cheap hotel, the scrabble of rats behind the walls of this cheap hotel, the bumps and thuds of the junkies on the roof of this cheap hotel. They all rise up, but I listen in between these sounds. In this hot dark room I strain for one particular noise, I listen for his footfall, I listen for his now familiar tread, knowing that at the first hearing I will have scant seconds to flee. It happened like this.

When one dines out as frequently as I used to, in the heady days when I was a star at home in England, there was one deeply irritating phenomenon which one often encountered – it was called 'splitting the bill'.

What invariably happened was that I'd be dining out with a large group of people in some pricey restaurant and all I'd have would be a glass of water and a small tomato while all the other greedy people I was with would have probably scoffed a whole baked warthog each. At the end of the meal one of the gluttons who'd had the Warthog *en Croûte* would shout 'Hey, let's not bother bickering about who's eaten what, let's just split the bill equally between us!' So I'd end up paying a hundred and seventy quid for a small glass of water and a Guernsey tom.

Almost a year ago now, on that fateful evening, I was with a large party of acquaintances at a fashionable Italian eaterie. Being a person of dainty appetite I merely sipped a glass of Lucozade and nibbled an organically grown turnip.

The rest of the group pigged on fine wines, rich meats and sweet cakes. When the bill came it was astronomical and, as usual, the greedy guts suggested we split it up equally.

Well I was buggered if I was going to pay a fortune for my meagre repast, so I decided to do something which I had not done since my mis-spent youth – I decided to 'Do A Runner' i.e. to leg it out of the restaurant without paying the bill.

Unfortunately as I was racing towards the door I was spotted by a waiter called Mario, who chased after me crying, 'Hey, fat signor, you no-a pay-a de check!' I got outside and leapt onto a passing number 38 bus, Mario flagged down a taxi and ordered it to follow.

At Victoria station I jumped off the bus and managed to buy the last ticket on the night train to Paris. Mario, fumbling with change to pay the taxi, missed the train by seconds. Instead he caught the Gatwick Express and boarded a late shuttle to Le Bourget Airport. He pounced from behind a pillar as I stumbled bleary-eyed through the early morning throng in the Gare du Nord. He was yelling 'You, you no-a-pay-a-your-bill, Mister!' I side-stepped, smacked him on the head with a croissant and ran.

In a scabrous absinthe bar in the depths of Montparnasse I signed on as entertainments officer on a tar-blackened tramp steamer laden with a cargo of Claire Bretecher books, bound for the souks of Tangiers. All was well until in the Gulf of Hammammet the look-out spotted a high-powered Zodiac launch racing through a cloud of spume towards us. Crouched over the twin 500cc Johnsons was Mario, muttering over and over to himself 'Service is not included mister, service is not included!' In a panic I dived overboard and swam towards the coast of North Africa. In Cairo he nearly had me and again in Harare, capital of Zimbabwe, I only just managed to escape from the suddenly strangely familiar Jehovah's Witness who approached me while I was dozing fitfully on a park bench.

Into Asia we chased. In a small mountain state high up in the oxygen-starved Hindu Kush I managed to convince the populace that I was a god by skilful use of a prophecy made long ago in their religion which stated 'And lo there will come a man, who has the ability to obtain substantial discount during sale time at a leading Knightsbridge Store'. One wave of my Harvey Nichols charge card and I was made king for life. When Mario inevitably turned up I had him thrown into the deepest dungeon.

Unfortunately the cunning swine conspired there with the leaders of the Kurdish minority to stage a *coup d'état* – I fled once more – just as the howling mob beat down the gates of my palace.

Now as I write, I am in this filthy bug-ridden hotel in the sleaziest part of Caracas. I listen for each footfall, each tread on the carpet, knowing that it will soon be him and again I will have to . . .

ARE YOU A MAN OR A MOUSE?
— SAID ALICE.

NOVEMBER

Right, he's wallowing in the bath eating a cornish pasty, the fat bastard. I've just got time to switch the envelopes before the messenger from *Time Out* comes. He'll go mad when he finds out I've switched columns, but it's really important! This vital information has come into my possession and he doesn't want me to share it with you. But I must. I really have to tell you!

Economic indicators – real clues to the true nature of our industry and commerce – are sought and consulted in the same way that ancient Romans stared at the insides of an ox hoping to find out how a battle would go. Exchange rates, trade deficits, sterling M3 index, are all supposed to let us know how we're doing economically, but there's a much better indicator – it's chocolate bars! Or rather the size of chocolate bars. If you think back to the boom times of the mid seventies, chocolate bars were titchy, scrawny little things. Mars bars were about the size of a small box of matches, Kit Kats were titchy and Aeros were almost all air bubble.

The theory behind it is that in times of economic boom, economic plenty, people buy chocolate bars as treats for themselves and are not concerned about food content or value for money. However when times get tough people want to be convinced that choccy bars are not greedy treats but are good food value and good value for money.

Thus with the recession in the late seventies and early eighties the size and weight of chocolate bars started to grow and grow, while the price dropped. Pretty soon Mars bars were the size of video cassette recorders and Aeros were as big as briefcases.

So you see if you really want to know how Britain plc is going, then just ignore the government propaganda about growth and instead take a look at the sweet counter. Now I don't want to worry anybody but I've just seen the first two-ton Crunchie!

One of the other awful things about the fat bastard is the terrible lies he tells. He said that all the hate letters about him were written by himself – the lying git! He gets so much hate mail the Post Office have given him his own postcode (W1A FAT1). Cop a load of the following taken at random from today's sack of nasty letters:

Dear Alexei,
Just give me the 20,000 and we can shake hands and be friends again.
Yours sincerely
H.M. Customs & Excise VAT Inspectorate

Dear Wacky-Man,
The Universality of the Faith has been a basic doctrine of the Roman Catholic Church since before the Council of Nicea. This doctrine has just been amended by the Encyclical *De Gustibus Malodorus Alexus Saylus*. The heathen, the heretic, the unbeliever are still welcome to repent and enter the fold of Mother Church – but not you. Quite simply, we don't want your sort. So if you're thinking of joining – get amnesiac. And I ain't whistling Matins, big boy.
Yours
The Pope (Managing Director, Cardinal Polish)

Dear Mr Big Bummer,
Just thought we'd better let you know you're not the best comic in the world. You're not even Good Value. You're not even Worth Thinking About.
Lots of love,
Which? Magazine

A SELF-PORTRAIT BY GERALD SCARF.

112

I love this autumnal time of year. The falling russet leaves hide all
the litter and the dead bodies and everything.

I am on a pilgrimage to a shrine, a shrine of comedy, located in
Monkseaton, Co Durham, home of 'Monkeaton's Own' Bobby
Chariot. Let me tell you some unpleasant facts about comedy and
comedians. Years ago one of the co-founders of the Comedy Store
(the club where I got my first Big Break), Peter Rosengard, decided
to start another club after falling out with his partner. He took
premises in Baker Street, London, and announced a grand opening
night. Reckoning I owed Rosengard something I agreed to put in a
mid-show appearance but said I wouldn't compère the show – which
had been my old function at the Comedy Store. Many people do not
realise that the compère is the most vital element of a good comedy
show. When I arrived, the M. C. that Rosengard had hired was
already up and performing – he was a fat club comic, with a battery of
old gags totally unsuited to the hip audience, he had a serious speech
impediment, he was sweating waterfalls of slime and he had about
him a stink reminiscent of the drains of Tangiers and worse than
that, the stink of failure. The evening was going badly.

I rushed up to the unfortunate Rosengard and said, 'Peter, where
the hell did you get this guy!?'

'Well,' said the quivering club owner, 'I rang up this leading
comedian and asked him who was his favourite comic and he said
this guy!'

Oh, Peter – BIG MISTAKE! What you have to understand about
comedians is that they are the most egotistical, sly, cunning, self-
centred individuals in the entertainment business which is saying
something. If an established comic should chance one night on a
young immensely talented performer in some half empty cabaret
they will not take that performer under their wing and nurture their
talent – they will instead go backstage and tell the tremulous
youngster how crap they were and tell them about the exciting
opportunities available in ten-year civil service administrative con-

113

tracts in Saudi Arabia. Similarly if you ask a comedian who their favourite comedian is they will sing the praises of some complete fuck-up because they DO NOT WANT THE COMPETITION!

The fact is that the comedian most admired, feared and worshipped by all other comedians is of course me! Yes – me. And how do you know it's Me? Because, of course, when asked in interviews who their favourite funny person is, all comics without exception mention somebody who isn't me! Simple deduction therefore reveals the truth.

Of course I am not as insecure as other comics. I can therefore reveal that my favourite stand-up is club comic Bobby Chariot. From his house in Monkseaton Bobby runs a comedy school – situated in Trevor Griffiths Boulevard in the Latin Quarter of Monkseaton. I am heading up there to do a few days guest lecturing, but for those of you who can't get to the school here are a few of Bobby's tips on comedy.

LESSON NINE: How to Write Jokes
1) Take a sharp pencil or biro and a clean sheet of paper.
2) Switch on the telly.
3) Wait until a comedy show comes on.
4) If a joke 'comes to you', write it down.
5) The *aide-memoire* for this lesson is 'TTP' – Turn on, Tune in, Pinch some Jokes.

LESSON ELEVEN: Funny Words (1)
The following words are funny. Try to get them into your jokes as much as possible: chicken, trousers, shoes, hat, cheese, lobster, tortoise, teapot, toolbox, tickling. Notice that several of them begin with the letter 'T'. A general rule is that words that start with the letter 'T' are funnier than others: tapioca, tango, tassel, texture. This is a general rule to which the word 'turpentine' is a notable exception. There is nothing funny at all about turpentine. If you've got a joke in your act about turpentine, forget it. It's a no-no.

What you must remember here is 'TTT' – Turkey, Tortoise, Trousers.

114

LESSON THIRTEEN: Shoes

The real key to great comedy is shoes. Many perfectly good acts have been ruined by shoes. The comic may be personable, the material solid, the timing excellent – but if the audience takes against the shoes you might as well go back to the insurance office. This piece of advice was given me by one who knows: Tommy Winstanley who was part-time Entertainments Manager at the Monkseaton Non-Aligned Left Club for nigh-on thirteen years. 'Shiny Oxfords make it every time, Bobby,' he used to say. 'Brogues and slip-ons might be acceptable on a younger class of comic, but show me a comic wearing suede on his feet and I'll show you a serious down-turn in the bar takings. I can't see how anybody could wear suede on their feet. It's soft to the touch for one thing. I can't abide things that are soft to the touch.' Tommy was, admittedly, a hard-liner when it came to shoes. He had a thing especially about Hush Puppies. In the end the seven comics, three jugglers and an eccentric dancer all wearing Hush Puppies and all nailed to the ceiling of the Monkseaton Non-Aligned Left Club became something of a tourist attraction.

The key to learning this lesson is 'EGBDS' – Every Good Boy Deserves Shoes.

LESSON EIGHT HUNDRED AND TWENTY-THREE: A Final Word.

Well, we've come to the end of our course of lessons and you should be ready, willing and, dare I say it, able to take your place in the hall of fame of professional comedians. Remember the key mnemonics:

'MTS' – Material, Timing, Smile;
'MSM' – Mirror, Signal, Manouevre;
'NUT' – National Union of Teachers.
'A+S=S' – Amibiton plus Shoes equals Success.
ITADLYSYSUYDR – If The Audience Don't Like You Smash Up Your Dressing Room.
'NAEEWWH' – Never Adjust Electrical Equipment With Wet Hands.
'RATS' – Remember About The Shoes.
Good Luck
God Bless
Bobby

KEN WAS TEMPTED BY
DOGMATISM.

DECEMBER

Merseyside Transport – No. 26 Sheil Road Circular.

I always go home to Liverpool at Christmas and it is a thrilling time
to be in that city – the population must almost double with the return
from afar of so many Scouse *'gastarbeiters'*.

Due to the economic decline of the North, the city of Liverpool
has witnessed a Diaspora – a scattering of its people – not seen on
such a scale since the Jews were driven out of Egypt. Over the past
ten years the population of the city has halved as its young men and
women have been forced to seek work where they can. The situation
is such that if you are perhaps approached by a Bedouin camel driver
near the ancient Jordanian city of Petra he will turn out on closer
examination to be an unemployed pipe-fitter welder called Billy
Dalrymple from Norris Green, Liverpool 5. Similarly many of the
sweat-shops of the Phillipines are now staffed by girls from the
estates of Huyton and Kirkby who are prepared to undercut the
wages of their oriental sisters. However, this emigration is not always
a gloomy story – for there is always the example of a young lad called
Ritchie Fletcher, who, when laid off from his job in a cake shop, went
abroad to seek his fortune and through hard work, enterprise and a
bit of luck eventually managed to have himself elected General
Secretary of the Communist Party of the Soviet Union and is now
the likely lad we all know as Mikhail Gorbachev. He's not the only
one either. I can remember when Robert Mugabe was a self-
employed plumber and part-time lead singer with the Merseybeat
group the St Louis Checks. I saw him down the Cavern one day
looking glum about the prospects of his continued employment.
'You're wasted at this game, Rob,' I said to him. 'Ere, have you ever
thought of leading a liberation struggle?' – the rest is history!

But one of the traumatic things that can happen when you go home at Christmas is when you go up to your old bedroom and find that your mother has had a 'clear-out'. And she's chucked out, or given away loads and loads of really special stuff that you'd had since you were a kid but just hadn't got round to moving.

In horror you find that your *Eagle* annuals have gone! Your model planes have vanished! Your teddy-bear is no more! Your train-set is missing! Your original rock and roll or soul records have disappeared!

Desperately you rush downstairs hoping against hope that Teddy has just been kidnapped by Basque separatists, you confront your Mum and smiling smugly she says, 'Oh all that old junk. I've given it to the bin-men,' or 'I've sent it to the children's hospital,' or 'I've burned it all' and you throw an absolute childish tantrum, rolling on the floor crying and biting the carpet and beating your fists on the floor even though you're now a forty-year-old professor of applied psychology.

And the most irritating thing is that you can't convince your Mum that some of that stuff that you've had since childhood is actually now really valuable and worth a lot of money. They smile at you as if you're still seven years old because to them it's just childish junk.

I was annoyed with my mother this Christmas because she threw out a load of stuff that I'd had in my bedroom for years. She gave the bin men two Leonardo drawings, a complete set of Chippendale chairs, an eighteenth century Adam fireplace and an original Gutenberg Bible.

When I said, 'Mum, some of that stuff was worth a lot of money!' She just smiled and said, 'Yes of course it was dear.'

If you're stuck for a Christmas gift this year then why not give a torch? A torch is a useful and elegant present, from the single cell plastic penlight to the mighty battery-chromed American monsters which throw a beam big enough to illuminate the planet Mars.

Many celebrities give torches to each other – Joan Collins has a box full of gold-plated bike lamps that she gives to close associates and Madonna buys Rolex and Cartier pocket torches for just about everyone.

If you'd like more information about the Exciting World of Torches then write to The Torch Information Council, The Battery, New York.

Ribble Bus Company: Route L59 – Liverpool to Ormskirk.

The only good thing about Christmas is that the post gets clogged up with all the Christmas cards and this helps to abate the endless flow of mail which comes every day addressed to me at the *Time Out* offices on the subject of eels. As regular readers of the column may know, a few months ago a small misprint in this column gave the impression that I was part-owner of a pet shop in Bristol and was an expert in the breeding, care and medical problems of eels. A full retraction was published the following week but to little avail. Every day another few sacks of letters arrive. For a time I took on a large staff of zoologists to deal with the letters but the expense proved to be crippling so I had to let them go back to the BBC at Bristol. Now, as well as I am able, I try to answer the letters myself.

> Dear Fatbastard,
> Should an eel wriggle all the time? Mine does. From when he gets up first thing in the morning to when he goes to bed at night he wriggles. He even wriggles a bit in his sleep. Is this normal or is he embarrassed about something?
> Yours in eeldom,
> Dennis P. Blowich, E6

Alexei replies: Dear Dennis, Fuck off.

> Dear Mr Sweary,
> I would like to buy my eel something tasteful but nice for his birthday. I thought of buying him a hat but he already has so many hats that he can hardly get them in his hat cupboard. A scarf is somehow too sensible. I'm sure you know what I mean. An electronic game springs to mind but I fear for the

119

underwater safety of such an object. He likes stationery but –
and here's the big one – could a rotary filing system have any
concealed dangers for an eel? I would hate to think of him
getting his fins trapped in a badly designed flange.
Yours truly,
Barry 'King' Dubois, SW12

Alexei replies: Dear Barry, Leave me alone.

Dear Mr Sayle,
What would you do with an uppity eel? Strangle the bastard?
Too right!
Yours comradely, Selina Scott

Alexei replies: Fuckoffandleavemealone.

Dear Alexei Sayle,
My eel is fond of fancy wall-light fittings. These, as you may
have noticed, usually take small candle-type light-bulbs. These
bulbs are not covered by the same British Standards
regulations as regular (full size) bulbs. The smaller bulbs 'go'
quicker, causing my eel a great deal of distress and expense. I
have got up a petition which several famous people have
already signed urging the government to set up a committee of
enquiry to look into this scandalous matter with the utmost
urgency. I trust I can count on your support.
Yours faithfully,
Ferdie the Lock-up Garage Man.

Alexei replies: Yes, yes, anything.

Dear Tom,
I'm sorry about the other night. I shouldn't have carried on that
way. It's just that for me the past no longer means very much. I
love Jerry. This is a fact you'll just have to face, I'm afraid. I
know how much it must hurt you but the sooner you can accept
that things have changed the better it will be all round. I've

120

tried not to love Jerry. I've tried and tried, but it's something that's completely taken me over and I seem powerless to stop it. At first I thought it was just a sexual thing, but it's not that. It's not just that he's infinitely better in bed than you are, he's also a much nicer person, better looking, better dressed, more successful, richer, more talented and not nearly as boring. I hope you won't take this personally. That's the way things are.

I wouldn't worry too much about what the hospital said about your tests. Senior Consultants often over-dramatise these things. I hope that Jacob and Emily are well. I'll be coming to visit them at the weekend as usual. I know it's difficult for you having to look after the children on a full-time basis and keep your twice daily appointments at the hospital but I'm sure you understand that Jerry's house is not really the right environment for children. The furniture is much too tasteful and expensive. Perhaps we can work out something more satisfactory in the fullness of time. If we can't, Jerry says he knows a Mr Garcia who can get a good price for them in Rio.

And don't worry about the eel. I've just written to Alexei Sayle, the eel specialist on *Time Out* magazine. If he can't sort out our problem, nobody can. I only hope I don't do my usual trick of mixing up the letters and the envelopes.
Keep Well,
I'm sorry,
Jen

Alexei replies: WAGA WAGGA WAGGA!!!!!

Dear Lexi,
Is it only eels you know about or do you know about beavers as well? It's not that I have got a beaver (yet!) but you never know, there may come the day when I find myself the possessor of as many as seven such industrious mammals – who knows what fate may have in store? And it would put my mind at rest if I knew there was somebody to whom I could turn for help and advice should such an eventuality occur. So, do you? If so,

would I really have to re-route a river through my flat just so they could dam it? This is what my friend says. He tells me that a beaver without a dam is an unhappy beaver and I would not like to cause any unhappiness. Some of my other friends say I look a bit like the late Bing Crosby. I enclose a photograph. What do you think?
Yours in God,
Monsignor Ben Cartwright

Alexei replies: Fuckofffuckofffuckofffuckofffuckoff fuckofffuckofffuckofffuckofffuckofffuckofffuckofffuckoff fuckofffuckofffuckofffuckofffuckofffuckofffuckofffuckoff fuckoff.

122

NEW YEAR'S EVE

So now it is the last day of my year of journeying. Many things have happened and some other things haven't happened. It is good to be back home and I have many parties to go to. Buses are hopeless at this time of year and only scum drink and drive so for the final chapter of this book we bring you:

GREAT MINI-CAB JOURNEYS OF THE WORLD

Being a Lenny Bruce-style confrontational comedian, it is my sacred duty to say the unsayable, to articulate those dreadful things which swim below the surface of the public consciousness, to voice opinions which are genuinely shocking. So now I will say something which some of you will find truly outrageous. I think London taxis are great! Yes, I know, but it's true. By and large as a regular user I have found the licensed black cabs courteous, honest, reasonably priced, clean, safe and uncannily good at navigating round London. However, as I'm also a regular cyclist I have frequently encountered cabbies' one dangerous and selfish act which is that they seem extremely reluctant to use their indicators. Maybe they are worried about the price of indicator bulbs, or perhaps the indicator switch is located in the boot – whatever the reason taxis are constantly switching lanes, doing U-turns, driving up walls, without giving any warning whatsoever. More than once this has caused me to indulge in cheerful cockney banter with cabbies.

ALEXEI (lying on floor): I say old man! Crikey! Be a bit more careful!

CABBIE: Gosh! I'm frightfully sorry old chap. I failed to indicate I was going to mount the pavement and drive through that doorway.

ALEXEI: Well, flipping heck, no harm done. But you should be more careful in future.

CABBIE: You're a toff sir. I most certainly will be. Cheerio!

However, if black taxis are usually good, the same is not always true of mini-cabs and mini-cab firms. As the great Chinese philosopher/poet Lao Shu wrote:

> Stars will always shine
> To light the way home
> Roots will always nestle
> In the dark brown loam
> Streams will always flow
> To fill the silver cup
> And your local cab firm
> Will always fuck you up.

You can do business with them for years, you can be godfather to the owner's children, you can have ordered the cab three years in advance and there will still come a point when you are waiting in the hall, bags packed, to catch a crucial flight and – no cab. You ring them up. They deny you exist. Rushing to the tube you knock over and kill a visiting alien from the Crab Nebula disguised as a tomato vendor. As a result angry aliens destroy the earth with a single beam from their mighty death star. It happens all the time.

Journey One.
Speedee Mini-Cabs. My House to Lambeth Palace for the Synod of the Church of England Feast of Bacchus Party.

Mind you I must say I'm not that fond of New Year's Eve. Chatting in a pub once to a gentleman called Tam who could, I think, be fairly described as a Scottish alcoholic – in fact he had it written under 'occupation' in his passport – emboldened by several pints I said 'Golly gosh, Tam. I bet you have a flipping jolly good time drinking at Hogmanay, don't you old chap?'

'Och naw!' shouted Tam, 'It's the woon night o' the year when I dinnae goo oot!'

124

'Gosh!' I replied, 'Given your liking for all things fermented I am quite taken aback. Why don't you go out on Hogmanay when everybody in your beloved Scotland is out having such a good time?'

Tam's face curled into a sneer terrible to behold and out of a mouth twisted with rage he spat: 'Och Hogmanay man! It's amatchoor 'oor.' I understood what he meant.

As a man who had given his life to the business of drinking and falling over, drinking some more, falling over again, without regard for the long hours or the arduous training required, he was infuriated by the sight of so many incompetent drinkers indulging in their once a year drunkness. In the same way as Nelson Piquet or Nigel Mansell might be annoyed to be confronted with a load of 1.6 Cavaliers and milk floats as they turned the straight at Silverstone.

Now cool people like myself and the fast crowd I run with feel the same way about Saturday night as Tam felt about Hogmanay.

While the common herd might get all dolled up and go out on a Samedi soir, the wild bunch that I hang out with – people like Gyles Brandreth, Benny Hill, Selina Scott, Toyah Wilcox, Mikhail Gorbachev etc. – get all dolled up in our best designer clothes and finest accessories and go out for a really good time only on a Tuesday morning at about 9.15. You see at that time all the bars and clubs aren't full of dull, dreary people from the suburbs. In fact all the bars and clubs are completely closed so we usually end up having a bun at a tea stall and then trying on all the gloves in British Home Stores until we get thrown out and have to go home.

Journey Two.

Lambeth Palace to Channel 4 cocktail party.

When you get into a taxi in Liverpool behind the dividing glass there is always an identity card, complete with photo of the face of the person who's supposed to be driving the cab.

Often the photo is definitely not of the geezer up front, but that's another story.

However, I reckon the licensing authorities have got it wrong anyway – surely the photo on the taxi driver's identity card shouldn't be of his face at all, it should be a nice big colour photo of the back of his head.

In fact further proof of the need for reform of this scandalous situation came to me recently. While riding in a Liverpool cab I got talking to the driver, a tall shaggy fellow.

He didn't say much but he seemed to have a sympathetic manner. So sympathetic in fact that I soon found myself pouring out, in an emotional torrent, my hopes, my fears, my darkest little secrets. Like why I'm frightened of grapefruit, for example.

It was only when, in floods of tears, I came to pay the fare that I realised that I'd been pouring out my heart to the taxi driver's Alsatian!

However, this story has a happy ending as the Alsatian is now studying to be a social worker.

Journey Three.

Channel 4 to Enfield Bus Garage, New Year's Eve brake fluid tasting party.

Holiday Questionnaire.

ARE YOU AN ALCOHOLIC?

1) How old are you?
   a) 18–25
   b) 25–40
   c) Tuesday

2) How much (on average) do you drink per day?
   a) I never drink
   b) I sometimes drink
   c) I already told you, it's Tuesday

3) When someone offers you a drink at a Christmas party, do you say:
   a) No
   b) Yes
   c) aaaaaaargh-hup-heeeeeeeeeeeee-whooooooooo

4) Some friends have called round unexpectedly for a game of bridge. You have no drink in the house. Do you:
   a) Offer them tea or coffee without apology
   b) Hurriedly rush round to the off license to stock up
   c) Think you're a yo-yo

5) A friend is about to leave your house and drive home. He/she is obviously over the limit. Do you:
   a) Offer to call a taxi
   b) Tell him/her jokily to watch out for the filth
   c) Suddenly remember a boy at school stealing the charm out of your lucky bag when you were six years old and weep inconsolably.

Journey Four.

Enfield to Deptford, Shotgun's Cocktail Bar.

Driver – Ralph from Deptford
Car – Beat-up Mark 1 Ford Granada

Synchro has gone on Ralph's forward gears so he prefers to drive backwards. Being a seasoned cab passenger I have a kit that I carry with me at all times. The most important part of this is a battery-powered light-up neon sign which reads – 'I'm a socialist. I neither agree with, nor endorse, the views of this driver. Please believe me. I am not a Nazi.' I used my sign quite often as Ralph yelled 'You Arab bastards!' at silly people who do not know we drive backwards on the right in this country.

127

Journey Five.

Abba Cabs, Deptford to Zanzibar Club, Covent Garden.

Car: Mercedes 500 SEL
Driver: Mehmet Alibar (Turkish Ambassador
to the Court of St James).

One of the social road-blocks of our age is that hiatus at the end of a dinner party or some other social occasion, between the ordering by phone of a cab and the cab's actual arrival. Spiritually, in that limbo-time, you have left the gathering while your body remains. Conversation becomes stilted and troubled and in the end everybody acts as if you have actually left. As long as the cab eventually turns up this remains a minor social embarrassment, but if the taxi fails to arrive at all, you can be in real trouble. Your friends will be compelled to act as if you are invisible. If asked they will deny your existence. Just like in that movie that everyone says is their favourite with James Stewart in it, the one they always show at Christmas and everyone cries where he wishes he's never been born and an angel comes from heaven – 'It's A Horrible Life' – that's the one.

My driver Mehmet was the Turkish Ambassador and was making extra cash on the side mini-cabbing with his official limousine. Like a lot of mini-cab drivers his knowledge of London geography was somewhat vague. Normally he would head for Chigwell where he had a cousin who owned a map of London printed on the side of a biscuit tin but luckily I had brought along my special 'Mini-Cab Driver's A–Z'.

While we drove I fell asleep on the floor and when I awoke we were outside a neat semi-detached house in Loughton Green. I have been in these situations before, delivered to some strange address by lost taxi drivers and it is easier to pretend that you live at the address you've been taken to rather than try and start all over again. Luckily the middle-aged couple who lived in the semi, Ron and Dorothy Harris, had a son Martyn who had disappeared after ordering a mini-cab to take him from a foam rubber exhibition at Olympia in 1984, so I moved into his room and will be marrying his fiancée Stacey at Saint Mungo's, Loughton early in the new year.

SPECIAL MINI-CAB
DRIVER'S A TO Z

Having had a few I slipped into a maudlin depression about New Year's Eve. I hate it really. Over the years I have developed several strategies to avoid the compulsory merriment.

STRATEGY ONE: Drink a lot of Mezcal. Mezcal is a Mexican drink distilled from the peyote cactus. It was reputedly first made by the Aztecs and played an important role in their religious rituals and spiritual life. Every bottle of Mezcal contains a 'worm' preserved in the spirit. The worm is, in fact, a species of grub, a common parasite of the peyote cactus. Eating the worm is said to enhance and prolong the 'enchantment' provided by the drink.

Although there are no 'rules' about such things, one of the traditional ways to drink Mezcal is with salt and lemon. You pour a generous measure of the drink and put a pinch of salt on the back of

129

your hand. Then you lick the salt, drain the glass and immediately chew a large slice of lemon. The drink itself is not as fiery or as rot gut as one would expect. It's as smooth as a good single malt whisky. It has a complex odour redolent of flowers and herbs. And it is most enchanting.

After one glass the cares of the world slip effortlessly from your shoulders. You relax and begin to see the world as a kinder, sunnier place.

After two glasses you are a king.

After three glasses you are a god.

After four glasses you are a sponge fisherman called Spiros. Every day you dive through the clear blue waters of the Aegean hunting the sponge. Although you are poor, so poor in fact that you cannot afford to buy the sponges which you catch and are forced to use a J-cloth, you are at peace with life. Your body is tanned and your hair black and shiny. You eat well: white bread and good olive oil and perhaps, if the week's labours have been fruitful and you have caught many sponges, a little meat on Sundays. You have a good heart, and although perhaps you sometimes drink a little too much of Christos's wine and raise a little hell, you do no real harm and Father Miklos sees no danger ahead for your immortal soul. But most of all you like to listen to Nicos, the old blind bouzouki player, and to dance the old dances and sing the old songs. You dance with spirit and with fire, turning every sinew of your body to the rhythm and the rise and fall of Nicos's bouzouki. And there is a passion in your voice when you sing the songs that sponge fishermen have sung since the days of your ancestors:

THE BIG SPONGE

You shall have ribbons, my pretty one
And an electric curling tong
You shall have these things to dress up your hair
When the big sponge comes along.

And you shall have good shoes from Saxones
That lace up with fine leather thongs

130

You shall have nice things to put on your feet
When the big sponge comes along.

'Marry a fisherman,' the old women say,
'And you certainly take a big plunge'
You might strike lucky
Or you might spend your life
Waiting, waiting for the big sponge.

You shall have a compact disc player
And your life shall be music and song
You shall have whitewash to put on your walls
When the big sponge comes along.

     After five glasses you get thrown out.

STRATEGY TWO: Mezcal is a Mexican drink distilled from the peyote cactus. It was reputedly first made by the Aztecs and played an important role in their . . . shit, we've done this one already . . . get back in the bottle you nasty little worm, you can't get me I'm a sponge fisherman.

STRATEGY THREE: disguise yourself as a frozen lasagne. Sure disguising yourself as a frozen lasagne is a lot of trouble but worth it for the peace and quiet of the big fridge at Sainsbury's all over the Bank Holiday. The only drawback to this one is the terrible cold and the problem that, if you don't get out fast on January 2 you might be sold to a couple called Paula and Mike who've invited another couple Trisha and Phil round for dinner. Paula and Mike don't like Trisha and Phil very much which is why they're giving them some frozen lasagne they bought from Sainsbury's. They won't tell Trisha and Phil it's frozen of course, they'll pretend that they've made it. I don't know why Trish and Phil and Paula and Mike carry on seeing each other. They don't like each other at all. They've all known each other since they were students at Sheffield University.
     Mike, in fact, used to go out with Trisha and there's still a slight frisson of jealousy between Paula and Trisha. When they first moved

to London, must have been in '78 or '79, they all shared a flat for a few months and things got very heavy because Paula wouldn't even go out to the shops if it meant leaving Mike alone in the flat with Trisha. Anyway, there's been a lot of water under the bridge since then, and about three or four years ago Mike, who was a social worker when he first left University, got this incredible job with this Market Research Company, and Paula's now a very high flyer in an independent production company that does a lot of training films and that sort of thing for big companies and might be doing a series for Channel 4, so Paula has to spend a lot of time having lunch with commissioning editors. Anyway, between them Paula and Mike are pulling something between 55 and 60K and that's not including the BMW Mike gets provided by the firm and all the other perks. And they've got this amazing house in Clapham and they were amongst the first people in the country to have a store card for Next Interiors so you can imagine – there isn't a wall in the entire house that hasn't been dragged, ragged or sponged and they make regular donations to the Greek Sponge Fishermen's Benevolent Association. And their door furniture alone must be worth thousands. And the trouble is that Trisha and Phil are still teachers and they live in a council flat in Dalston that they were lucky to get really, and Phil still drives that bloody 2CV that he's had for years and it's horrible when you go round to their flat because you have to listen to Sade on cassette for God's sake because they can't even afford a CD and once you've got used to listening to Sade on CD, cassettes just sound like a bloody joke, don't they? And they've only got the one Sade cassette and they haven't got any Suzanne Vega at all so when the Sade's finished you have to listen to Phil's antique Steely Dan records which sound as if they're kept in the sugar basin. And it's not like Mike and Paula to flaunt their money but it's just that Trisha and Phil make them feel that they do. And what can you talk about? I mean if you've spent the last three weeks choosing a border paper to go under the dado in the spare room and you meet up with some old friends, you want to share the experience with them, don't you? Even though you spend more in a week on border paper than they do in a year on bloody wine by the taste of it. And if Paula and Mike did give Trisha and Phil anything decent to eat like that new recipe for corn-fed chicken and watercress sauce that Paula got out of 'Options' rather than frozen lasagne, Trisha and Phil would only secretly think that Paula and Mike were flaunting their money again. So what's the point? And won't they all be surprised when, in the middle of the dinner party, their lasagne jumps off the plate and reveals his true identity?

THE QUEEN'S AWARD FOR... CAPITALIST EXPLOITATION.

JANUARY THE FIRST

A new year dawns, cold and clear. It is good to be back home. No buses run today and it is good for I shall not take another for a while. This first day of the year is a day for reflection and after much thought I have made but one new year's resolution:

'No More Mr Nice Guy.'

A.S. & D.S.
221B Baker Street,
Kidderminster.
January.

GREAT CLASSICS OF BADLY PRINTED FICTION

IN YOUR OWN HOME FROM...

THE MISPRINT LIBRARY.

'LADY CHATTERLEY'S GLOVER': Life changes for Lady Chatterley when she discovers that her gamekeeper, Mellors, can also knit mittens.

'THE FORSYTE SAGO': The story of a family, an inheritance and a milk pudding.

'GREAT EXPECTORATIONS': Young Pip meets Magwich the convict near his home one night and helps him. Magwich subsequently becomes Pip's secret benefactor and gives him enough to go to London and learn to spit.

'MOBY DUCK': The allegorical tale of Captain Ahab and his hunt for a giant white killer quacker.